*don't
leave
yet*

don't leave yet

HOW MY MOTHER'S
ALZHEIMER'S
OPENED MY HEART

CONSTANCE HANSTEDT

SHE WRITES PRESS

Published 2015
Printed in the United States of America
ISBN: 978-1-63152-952-8
Library of Congress Control Number: 2014947116

For information, address:
She Writes Press
1563 Solano Ave #546
Berkeley, CA 94707

She Writes Press is a division of Spark Point Studio, LLC.

For my sister,
Judy Cahill

And in memory of my mother,
Virginia Cheslock
October 16, 1923–April 22, 2008

I often wondered if my mother dreamed in earth tones. My dreams heralded sparkling blues and greens, not simply water and seaweed, and, although she had a penchant for beige, I wanted hers to be just as alive. Landscapes seared a lustrous gold. Tangerine bursts through the trees.

When my sister and I began inventorying Mom's belongings on an August Monday morning, I reeled with the thought that perhaps she never dreamed at all, day-to-day life being more than enough to handle. Gloomily, I positioned my laptop on her Ethan Allen dining room table and turned it on. An empty spreadsheet loomed before me.

Three months had passed since we'd placed Mom in an assisted-living center, and throughout the summer I'd envisioned myself here: walking from one cream-colored room to another, opening windows she rarely cracked because of allergies and a peculiar aversion to fresh air, feeling the breeze off the neighbor's cottonwoods, and recalling the irritation in Mom's voice when their sticky white residue clung to her stately poplars and evergreens.

Even the memory of how she never closed her drapes to blistering noontime sun or deep black of evening caused me to miss her terribly, and there wasn't a damn thing I could do about it.

"Toaster, steam iron," Judy called from behind the louvered door of the kitchen pantry. "And what looks like a brand-new can opener."

"I doubt she ever used it," I said, flipping the switch of the brass light fixture above me and typing the items into the left column of my spreadsheet. "She didn't buy my idea about a steam iron being more convenient, either." I pictured Mom topping a water-filled Pepsi bottle with something resembling a showerhead, sprinkling our freshly laundered clothes, and rolling them like breadsticks until they were ready to iron.

Judy laughed, before appearing with a square Tupperware stuffed with Saltines. Her eyes widened, sending her thick brows a quarter of an inch above her mauve wire-framed glasses. "Jeez, Con, what did she live on?" She threw the container down and reached back in for two red-labeled cans. "Campbell's tomato soup? Chicken noodle? 'Pitiful,' as Bill would say."

Our brother's favorite expression was an apt description. When Judy and I had cleaned out Mom's refrigerator in May, we'd been amazed by its miserable contents. Not counting condiments, there hadn't been much more than a few shriveled oranges, American cheese slices, and Oscar Mayer bologna. Then I understood how Mom had dropped twenty pounds since Christmas.

My stomach churned at the image of her living alone since our father had died, seven years earlier. My husband, Gary, our two children, and I visited her in Wisconsin almost every summer, and she traveled twice a year to our home in California. Although she had never been socially inclined, her activity outside the dark brown ranch house on Palisades Lane had been reduced to grocery shopping, an occasional lunch with a former coworker, and her monthly poker club.

Even though Mom wasn't a social butterfly, she disliked not being included and hated the ensuing loneliness. Still, my siblings and I couldn't persuade her to consider other living arrangements. I'd asked her if she wanted to move by me, or at least to a condominium with less upkeep and the possibility of making new friends. But she'd waffled, and at age seventy-seven had stubbornly stuck to her schedule of housework and lawn care, viciously shampooing shag carpeting in spring, trimming bushes into neat pillars in summer, and raking mounds of burnt-orange leaves during autumn. She was obsessed with leaves; they clogged the eaves and swirled defiantly over her large yard. I was grateful when the first snow fell in the Fox River Valley so I didn't have to hear her complain.

As Judy moved on to a cupboard, counting water glasses and coffee cups, I recalled my conversations with Mom earlier in the year. In January she'd remembered Bill's birthday yet hadn't been able to determine his age.

"Now, if Judy is fifty—"

"No, Mom," I'd interrupted. "Judy's fifty-four."

"Oh, right."

I imagined her perched on the olive-plaid love seat in the finished half of her basement, erasing her mistake like a schoolgirl at a dusty blackboard. When she concluded that Bill was eighteen months younger than Judy, I chalked up her miscalculation to lack of sleep, since cars supposedly careened down her street all night.

During February, we'd planned for her visit at Easter. "If I'm feeling better," she'd said.

"What's wrong?" I'd asked, anticipating her stock answer. Complaints of stomachaches, headaches, even tingling in her feet had become quite regular.

"I'm sure *I* don't know."

"In that case, call your doctor. We don't want anything to spoil our good time." I recalled an egg-dyeing scene from when my son, Ryan, was around ten. Spooning vinegar water over a hard-boiled egg, he asked, "Is this done, Grandma?" Before she could reply with her usual "It most certainly is," he dipped it a minute too long and the butter yellow succumbed to a splotchy mustard. Mom then showed him the "correct" way to color a beautiful egg.

To talk to her in the following months, I had to place the calls, since, rather oddly, she'd stopped contacting me altogether. When my kids were small, the phone rang at nine o'clock every Saturday morning. As they got older and Ryan played baseball and Cara figure-skated, I began to say, "Mom, we'll reach you" or, "Try at lunch, when we're sure to be home." But my suggestions, like countless others, didn't make a dent in her routine.

Suddenly, Mom's Easter visit took on new importance. I felt like a lousy daughter, and nurse, from two thousand miles away.

"Connie, are you listening?" Judy repeated now, stretching her five-foot-two-inch frame to reach the top shelf, the collar of her rose polo grazing her short gray hair.

"What? How many serving plates?" I couldn't believe I was asking this question, or that Mom no longer lived in her house of twenty-five years. Taking inventory of what remained of her lean existence for an estate auction was a job I'd never anticipated, and one, I realized, for which it was impossible to prepare. I was certain I couldn't do it without Judy.

I was enduring an OSHA safety seminar in San Jose the day before Mom's visit in April. When the instructor switched off his microphone for a welcome fifteen-minute break, I paced the Hilton's jade-carpeted hallway and called Mom on my cell phone. She hadn't been feeling well on Saturday—diarrhea again, she'd explained. So I decided to check in and finalize my plan to pick her up at the Oakland airport.

She answered the phone with a flat, uninterested "hello," followed by a sigh. I cringed at her tone.

"So, are you all packed?" I asked, trying to sound excited. It was a chore Mom began days in advance, arranging blouses and socks in tall piles on her bedroom floor. I pictured plastic bags with face creams and lotions and wire hangers readied for action in my guest room closet.

"I'm sick!" she began. "Ate some soup for lunch—"

"Wait a minute," I said quickly. "What do you mean?" Sensing our conversation was going to swallow my entire break, I settled into a well-used, overstuffed chair by the elevator. I braced myself.

"I don't think I can come, Connie. I haven't packed. I asked Rita and Don to help me put some things together, but they had to go play *bingo*." The weakness in her voice did nothing to hide her disdain.

I couldn't imagine Mom asking anyone for help, especially her youngest sister and husband. Although they lived a mile from her Palisades neighborhood, they'd reconnected only recently after years of infrequent visits.

"Did you get through to the doctor yet? You have to, if you have constant diarrhea. And make sure you tell the nurse you want to speak to *him*."

According to Mom, this particular woman could be as impenetrable as the Berlin Wall. On a good day, Mom was capable of being a worthy adversary; she knew how to get her way. This time, I wasn't so sure.

"Okay, I'll try," she whimpered. "I'm really sorry, Connie."

After promising to hear how she fared during the noon hour, I walked back to the conference room, sluggish from the weight of her anxiety and my confusion. I wanted nothing more than to leave my lecture notes and drive home to the comfort of my bedroom. My daydream shattered, however, as the instructor annoyingly tapped the microphone and announced his next topic.

While I was growing up on State Street, my family was the only one I knew in which both parents were employed. They worked at the same printing company, located on the "island" just over the Main Street Bridge. The bridge, and the Fox River below it, divided our town of fifteen thousand into the rich people on the island and the rest of us, who lived north of the waterway.

Because both my parents worked, some of my friends thought we had more money than they did. It certainly didn't feel that way, since we lived in similar compact houses. Nothing about us was fancy: I wore Judy's hand-me-downs until junior high; we didn't own a boat, like the islanders did; and our Ford was practical for a family of five, when "traveling" meant loading the car in summer with sandwiches and pop and driving two sweaty hours to Aunt Rosemary and Uncle Gene's in Waukesha.

My parents saved for my siblings and me to attend college—a rare occurrence in our town when they were young. "If only Daddy had let Rosemary go off to school, she would have done quite well for herself," Mom had said of the man who didn't believe in higher education for women. Although she never indicated such a desire for herself, I wondered if she would have followed in her older sister's footsteps. Yet managing a stenography department, with its attention to details and deadlines, suited her fiery command for perfection.

I loved watching Mom's morning ritual. In front of her bedroom mirror, she applied pale pink lipstick and sprayed Clairol on her bouffant, a medium brown accented by a frosty streak just above her forehead. Then, with determined efficiency, she zipped up a navy knit, cinched its belt, and slipped on silver bangles.

Occasionally I was allowed to visit her second-floor office. Her desk overflowed with papers, red pencils for correcting "careless" mistakes, and African violets. At other desks positioned around the room, young women snapped Juicy Fruit while tapping their polished nails on typewriter keys. When Mom told them chewing gum was too distracting, they immediately reached for tissues.

Dad ran a letterpress on the first floor, his shift alternating every week. I preferred the seven-to-three shift so we could all gather around the black-and-white Zenith after supper, Dad looking especially tired as he sank into his easy chair. More important, his presence after school protected me from my brother's inclination to spin me around on the nubby gold couch like a cone of cotton candy.

When Dad worked three to eleven, my siblings and I were on our own, the hierarchy having been established early on. Although Judy and Bill were close in age and I was four years younger, Judy's job was to maintain order, which she did by holing up in our shared bedroom, listening to Johnny Mathis records. Meanwhile, Bill and I overturned chairs and stacked cushions in the living room for rubber-band fights. He was an excellent marksman, and I did my best to hide how much it stung, soaking my battle wounds later under streams of cold water.

Dad's other shift, eleven at night until seven the next morning, was the one we dreaded most. Mom insisted on quiet play after homework so Dad could sleep, an almost impossible task in our tiny house. But we did as we were told, stretching out on Bill's hardwood floor with Monopoly or Easy Money after tiring of TV. I, for one, had no intention of misbehaving; Mom's short temper was nothing to mess with.

One summer after school let out, Dad's coworkers in the pressroom threatened to go on strike. "They're trying to do what's best for their families, Virginia," Dad explained, his red hands squeaking across the soapy supper dishes.

"Well, they should be grateful they *have* a job," Mom said, stacking the plates I dried in the cupboard.

A steamy rinse of the sink ended their discussion. I crawled into bed, wishing I could wake in the morning like my friends, with a mother flipping pancakes as if she had all the time in the world, and a father pecking her cheek before he left for work.

When my seminar broke for lunch, I hurried to my car in the parking lot across the street. The inside was suffocating. I rolled down the windows and dialed Mom's number. She picked up on the first ring. I imagined her leaning on a kitchen counter, as close as possible to the beige wall phone so as not to stretch its cord.

"I've decided not to chance it," she said with conviction. "I don't want any problems at the airport."

"Did you speak to the doctor?"

"He told me to make another appointment. It's hopeless, Connie. Week after week I'm the same. He can't help me."

I swallowed hard and straightened in my seat. "Did you tell him about the diarrhea?"

"I don't know! What difference does it make?"

"You want to feel better, don't you?"

"It doesn't matter," she said limply.

"*Listen*, Mom, and don't argue. Call him again. Say you need to talk to someone about your anxiety. All right? I'll expect to hear an answer."

She offered a weak "okay" and hung up. I lay back and wiped my damp forehead, amazed I hadn't minced words. She disliked being told what to do and released her frustration on anyone who tried. I was still learning how to stand up to my mother.

Now I wondered what else could be done. Judy and Bill weren't close by, either; they lived in Illinois and Florida. However, they'd shared my growing concern this past year, especially Judy, as we'd raised our record for a phone call from two hours to three. I pressed her speed-dial button.

"It doesn't surprise me she's not coming," I said tiredly.

"But it's odd she waited until today to tell you. I swear, she gets rattled to the point where she *makes* herself sick. I think Bill's had her pegged all along."

As a psychiatric RN for a dozen years, Bill stuck to his diagnosis of our mother: acute depression with tendencies of paranoia. When the three of us discussed our lives on State Street, we knew it had been considerably longer than that.

As far back as I remembered, I was my mother's favorite child. "God blessed me the day you were born," she repeated each time she visited. "Unlike Judy and Bill, your sole purpose in life wasn't to drive me crazy."

"Oh, they couldn't have been *that* bad," I said as she opened her suitcase, found a bag of M&M's, and tossed it to Ryan. Mom brought gifts for him and Cara whenever she came.

"They locked me in the attic on 7th Street while I was cleaning! From the window I saw four-year-old Judy and Bill, wearing only a diaper, run around the house, laughing like hyenas. Luckily, the neighbor was hanging laundry in her backyard and heard me scream."

"They were being kids, Mom."

"And since Dad took our car to work, I pulled them in the wagon to the store. In the winter, too. Of course, Bill couldn't just ride. He scaled snowbanks and sloshed in every puddle in sight. By the time we reached Red Owl, he was soaking wet and people glared at me like I was a bad mother."

I noticed Ryan stifling a laugh with his hands. Mom looked at him, too, and added, "But your mother was different. Quiet, well behaved."

Submissive, I wanted to say yet didn't. And even something more. It was as if I'd been born in fear. Excessively watchful and vigilant. I saw the anger Mom unleashed on my siblings and learned early on to obey and hold my tongue. One slip might take days or weeks to undo, before we were welcomed again into the folds of her plump, lotioned arms. Being her youngest was hard work; I did everything I could to stay in her good graces.

I recalled taking a bowl of Bing cherries from the refrigerator and banging a corner of the oven door. So easy to do, I reasoned, since the harvest-gold appliances stood side by side, separated by inches. Mom, always on guard for catastrophe, ran into the kitchen and gasped.

"How clumsy," she said, fingering the coffee-colored gash. "Money down the drain to have it replaced."

"It was an accident," I mumbled, without looking up.

My words did little to soothe her. She retold the story at supper while I sank into my chair like a criminal. From then on, I was anxious whenever I opened the refrigerator. When the oven door was replaced a week later and I hit that one, too, I gave up trying to defend myself. It felt safer to agree with whatever she said, even if the tiny black dots in her eyes bore holes right through me.

At four thirty the screen behind the overhead projector turned white. I stretched my arms, unhinged my back, and quickly headed out.

I wasn't sure which was worse, facing the heavy commute or making the last call of the day. I didn't doubt Mom was sick. What troubled me was the distinct difference in her voice: unsteady and weak, each word expelled with hesitation.

"Connie, what should I do?" she asked when she picked up. I pictured her rubbing her forehead, the skin pink and raw from worry.

"Let's talk tomorrow. Why don't you put on your nightgown and crawl into bed?"

It was the best I could do. I said good-bye and turned on the ignition, relishing a blast of cold air. There was no sense in hurrying, since the freeway toward home would be backed up for at least five miles. I sat in the growing shadows of the parking lot and wondered if Judy could drive from Chicago to check on Mom. It seemed inconceivable that our stubborn, independent mother had run out of answers.

2

"This is it!" Judy exclaimed, pointing to the right and final side of the kitchen. I pressed "save" on my laptop and stood next to her, eager to sift though the everyday items in what Mom referred to as her "junk" drawer. A faded Sucrets tin jingled with safety pins and buttons. Ballpoint pens advertised Twin Cities Savings and Loan. Coupons for a local car wash cited expiration dates from months ago.

"You can't even tell she *lived* here!" I said. "I don't know what I expected, but no notes, no shopping lists?"

"I've got a hunch she's been busy," Judy said flatly. "The garage on the way in this morning looked pretty bare-bones, too. Why did she throw so much away? I thought people who lived through the Depression saved a lot of stuff."

"Has Mom ever been like other people?" I recalled her rummage sale on State Street before she and my dad had moved here, when everything our parents owned had been up for grabs: Chairs, lamps, and tables sported tie-on price tags upstairs; dishes and knickknacks with stick-on silver dots covered the Ping-Pong table in the basement. Sentimentality never entered the picture as crystal wedding goblets were carried out the door one by one.

Judy closed the drawer and opened the cupboard below it. "Ah, but she did save the Candlewick, and she's always meant for you to have it."

Ever since I was a girl, I'd heard how the crystal-beaded plates, cups and saucers, relish trays, and champagne glasses would one day be mine. They were by far Mom's most valuable possessions, and for me the strongest physical connection to the house where I grew up.

I always knew when supper was special: Mom got down on her hands and knees to retrieve the Candlewick and announced dinner would be served at five sharp. She did this every Christmas Eve, whizzing from cutting boards to saucepans to prove her theory that preparation was key.

"Let's see. The turkey needs more browning. I'll slice the apples, bananas, and oranges for the salad now and whip the cream later. Oh, and warm the dinner rolls. Can't forget those. They're your dad's favorites."

Somehow Mom maintained order amid the chaos. Judy and I tried to help but, unless assigned specific jobs, stood silently in place so as not to disrupt her.

The best part of the day, next to unwrapping one present after dessert, was watching her set the table. Every movement had a precise purpose: pull open a drawer for the linen tablecloth, then cover the Formica just so; count napkins and silverware and arrange alongside the Candlewick; remove cranberries from the refrigerator and place strategically between the meat platter and the bowl of green beans; light two red tapers and switch off the overhead fluorescent. It was magic.

No other moment in our house on State Street was as calm. Polite conversation and "please pass the potatoes" manners felt like just rewards for the frantic days leading up to Christmas, when tempers flared as regularly as car tires spinning on icy streets.

"Ed, move that damn tree!" Mom yelled after Dad plopped the grocery-store pine into its stand. "It's leaning on the window!"

"I *am*, Virginia. I'd like to see you do better."

"Well, I could do a hell of a lot . . . God, now it's hitting the ceiling! Drag that thing outside and cut more off."

"You want it shorter, you do it."

"Oh, that's right—stomp out and leave me with this monstrosity.

Show the kids what a help you are. I always have to do everything myself."

I sank into the farthest corner of the couch, clutching Judy's sweaty hand. Bill sat tall and still like the altar boy he portrayed at Sunday Mass.

"Okay, kids, is this its best side? Is it straight?"

We didn't answer. My voice hid deep inside my throat, where I intended it to stay. Mom complained bitterly about the "ugly" tree the entire time she strung gold lights and garlands. When she asked, "Who wants to hang the bulbs?" we hesitated, certain that no matter how carefully we searched among the prickly limbs, she'd question our chosen spots. "Don't you think that's too high?" "Let's not crowd them together."

Yet at the end of the night Mom proclaimed the tree "beautiful." I nodded, thankful the task was done. As I settled between my pale yellow sheets in the twin bed next to Judy's, I wondered how long the peace would last.

It felt strange knowing the Candlewick dishes were now mine. It was too early. I envisioned myself older and grayer, cooking Thanksgiving dinner for my own grandchildren, explaining that the giblet stuffing was their great-grandmother's recipe. They'd beg to light the candles and swoon at my iced cookies on the dessert tray.

That scenario had disintegrated, and Judy and I never saw it coming.

"Mom's always been self-centered," Judy said matter-of-factly, approaching the hutch behind the dining room table. "Her behavior didn't seem any different from normal."

I agreed and labeled a new page. "Except for being obsessed with the what-ifs: if the furnace will break down, if the roof will leak. I should have known more was going on. I could have asked questions, stomached her snide remarks. If I'd seen how thin she was, how little she ate . . . Well, it seems so easy *now*, doesn't it?"

The morning sun attained its noontime position, leaving the living room to our left dark and drab. The brass tea set on the glass table appeared tarnished, the Oriental rug faded and frayed. I felt stiff with guilt, the forty-eight-year layering of having been an imperfect daughter. In many ways I was still the same blond girl, reaching for the hand of her loving big sister.

I never heard Dad leave on Saturday nights. After soaking in a bubble bath and popping into pajamas, I'd realize he was gone. The rest of us watched *Lawrence Welk*, Judy and I singing along with the Lennon Sisters while Mom ironed. Once, when Judy was on a date and Myron Floren was playing his accordion, a ruckus outside startled us. Mom, Bill, and I raced to the kitchen window overlooking the driveway and saw Uncle Florian dragging Dad by his shirtsleeves toward the back porch.

Mom whipped open the door and screamed, "How can you show up like this!"

I couldn't believe the limp creature now sprawled on the gray linoleum was my father, groaning over and over, "Leave me the hell alone." Yet, amazingly, in the next instant he stood, wobbling like a bowling pin and raising his arms high into the air to meet his brother's. Terrified, I hid behind Bill. They grunted and struggled down the length of the hallway, Florian pinning Dad to the wall by his bedroom.

Mom sobbed, "I should have called Tony's sooner."

Taverns were big draws on weekends. According to Mom, their patrons were immoral and disgusting. Florian was already in their ranks, being a regular. Now Dad was one of them. I felt queasy. The popcorn I had eaten earlier rolled in my stomach like gravel in a concrete mixer.

"Don't worry, kids. He's okay," Florian slurred, forcing Dad through the doorway. As Bill and I tiptoed back to the couch, I knew nothing could have been further from the truth. My heart sank when Florian reappeared and timidly waved good-bye.

After several minutes, we heard a loud crash. "I bet Dad fell off the bed," Bill whispered. Bravely, we peeked into the hall. Their door was shut. The velveteen rocker, which normally sat next to Mom's tall walnut dresser, had been wedged into a corner. The sharp mixture of vomit and carpet cleaner hung in the air.

"It's all right," Bill said. I shuddered and snuck into my room. No matter how far I dug under the covers, I couldn't drown out the swear words coming from the other side of my wall. I prayed for Judy to return early, yet hours passed before her nyloned feet crossed our wood floor. By then the house was quiet.

At breakfast the following morning, Dad ate in silence while Mom slammed cupboards with a vengeance. "Girls, tell your father what you think of his behavior last night."

Judy didn't look up from her eggs over easy. As Dad sighed heavily in the chair next to mine, I didn't dare open my mouth. I longed to be invisible. And I ached deep inside for betraying my mother.

The day after the safety seminar, I sat in my office, mulling over Mom's question: What *should* she do? More important, it was Wednesday, three full days before Judy could drive north.

Fortunately, Gary's parents lived a few blocks from Mom. If something was terribly wrong, I could count on Bev and Al. To be on the safe side, I asked them to pay her a visit. They reported that even though it had been only six o'clock in the evening, Mom had answered the door in her nightgown. I wondered if she was getting out of bed at all.

On Thursday Mom said she had called her doctor. "We went over the crap I'm taking: Prozac, Ativan, Linoxin."

I wrote furiously on my notepad until it hit. "Prozac?"

"It's been several months already."

"Well, I'm surprised he didn't recommend a psychiatrist." I could hardly believe I'd finally said it out loud. Oddly, she didn't object. I blew air from my lungs until my chest felt nearly weightless.

We hung up, and my extension rang five minutes later. "Connie, I told the nurse your idea. She thinks it's a move in the right direction. Why didn't someone suggest this sooner?"

"We have, Mom. You wouldn't listen."

In fact, she'd made it explicitly clear since Dad died that she never wanted to hear the word *depression*. Bill's career might as well have been in used-car sales, for the little respect Mom showed him. Yet it was troubling that her own doctor hadn't done more, since she'd called 911 numerous times and made at least half a dozen trips to the emergency room with so-called breathing problems.

On Saturday, a couple of hours before Judy's arrival at Palisades Lane, I answered the phone to Mom's hysterical sobs.

"I smell gas in the house! Al sniffed around the furnace, but he claims it's fine. A friend said maybe there's a leak, since I always feel sick. So I had the gas company come."

"And?"

"They didn't find anything. God, Connie, I can't live here anymore! I'd rather be dead."

"Mom, get a hold of yourself. We'll get this straightened out."

My father-in-law dropped by again that day, as did a neighbor, concerned by the presence of the gas truck. No one could calm Mom's frazzled nerves. I felt my own panic rising; we were running out of options.

While waiting for Judy's call, I scrubbed sinks and showers, lugging a Sony boom box, along with Lysol, from one bathroom to the next. I listened to the A's game, longing to be among the thousands in the stands at the Oakland Coliseum. What I wouldn't have given for a Corona and nachos, a hot dog drenched in ketchup.

"Brass candlesticks, two. Brass pots, three," Judy continued, "counting the one with the dead ficus."

I typed in the numbers while contemplating Mom's decorating style. After she and Dad had moved here from State Street, she'd discovered an Ethan Allen store and claimed its interior designer was the only person with good taste. Fran, in fact, could do no wrong.

"She suggested this Oriental rug," Mom said when I visited. "I love it—so elegant yet homey."

I looked skeptically at the brown-and-gold mammoth consuming the open space of the living room.

"Fran says it makes a statement."

To me it blared, *I'm here to impress you because I'm expensive,* but I kept my opinion to myself. Mom had furnished her entire house under Fran's supervision. Each vase, ginger jar, and print on the wall came from the caverns of Ethan Allen. Then, as if she were Fran's protégée, she'd say, "Connie, maybe you should consider a fruit centerpiece for your table."

Of course, she meant the waxy, artificial kind, and I couldn't think of anything more impractical.

"Then how about grapes hanging in a wall container? Did you see mine in the guest room?"

I glared at her. "Not happening."

Over time, Christmases and birthdays brought an accumulation of brass and pewter as Mom attempted to improve the style of my homes. "Pick out what appeals to you," she'd say during our once-a-year Ethan Allen tours, and I'd reluctantly search through their elaborate displays. When I finally chose a pillow or serving tray I was sure I'd use, Mom squealed with delight and proudly announced my decision to a sales associate.

My mother was always a woman in charge. On the night before baking Christmas cookies in our yellow kitchen on State Street, she prepared the dough, mixing eggs, butter, sugar, flour, and nutmeg with her wooden spoon as intently as a wizard stirring a magic potion.

"Your turn, Connie," she said. "Scrape all the flour off the sides of the bowl. There, you're doing it."

When I thought she wasn't looking, I swiped my finger under the rim and then across my tongue.

"How is it?" she asked.

I detected satisfaction in her voice and answered, "Perfect." Everything was. We wore matching blue-checked aprons, and I had her undivided attention. There was a lightness about her. She appeared cheerful, invigorated, and uncharacteristically patient. This was my mother at her best.

The next morning, Judy and I sorted cookie cutters while Mom rolled the chilled dough on the breadboard. "One quarter of an inch, no more, no less," she explained. "Quickly, too, before it warms and sticks to the rolling pin. Now, Judy, set the Christmas-tree cutter near the edge. Press down . . . carefully lift up . . . good. Drop it on the baking sheet."

Since my attempts produced mostly unrecognizable shapes, I watched as my mother and sister arranged bells, stars, and wreaths in neat rows. Mom insisted on using all the animal-shape cutters as well, even though Judy and I wondered what bunnies, chickens, and horses had to do with the holiday. Yet we were allowed to eat any broken legs and heads, as was Dad, who'd appear in the doorway every so often, asking for "casualties."

After lunch Mom blended powdered sugar, Carnation, and butter with the electric mixer, then spooned the frosting into cereal bowls, adding dabs of red and green food coloring. Judy and I uncapped containers of multicolored sprinkles and taped waxed paper to the table, in front of four chairs. "Bill, come help!" we yelled.

Once we were in our positions, Mom made her annual plea. "Kids, not too much candy. Nothing is worse than biting into a cookie loaded with junk. Bill, what did I say? Shake some off."

He grinned and popped it into his mouth.

"Not another one!" she scolded while cracking a smile.

"I'm testing them. Besides, you didn't like it. You hate all of mine."

Mom rolled her eyes. "Sparse cookies look and taste the best."

Predictably, however, Judy had the right touch. Her gingerbread men came to life: Chocolate drops shoed their feet, thick frosting belted their waists, and red hots formed their faces. "Isn't she clever?" Mom gushed. It was hard to compete with her "creative" child. Bill and I studied our cookies, clearly in a dead heat for distant runner-up.

An hour after the A's had chalked up another loss to the Yankees and I'd finished mopping the bathroom floors, Judy called from Mom's house.

"What a horrible day. Thank God Bev was here, or I might have jumped ship."

"What happened?" I asked, dropping onto my bed.

"Oh God, where to begin?" She gulped air like a long-distance swimmer before taking the first plunge. "Mom was a mess. Bev said she cried all afternoon about the damn furnace."

I was baffled. "Even after the gas company checked it?"

"Uh-huh." The sarcasm in those two tiny syllables was palpable. I leaned back against my pillow and stared at the high ceiling. In a corner was a crack I'd noticed several weeks before, longer now, fish-line straight and black. I closed my eyes when Judy continued, and pictured Gary on an eight-foot ladder with a putty knife.

"I asked Mom if she'd taken her Ativan, and she rocked back and forth on the couch: 'I don't know, I don't know.' I've never seen her so unglued, Con."

My mind shifted, and I saw them in my mother's living room, the crystal table lamp casting a soft glow on their anxious faces. "I can't imagine," I said.

"I suggested Pizza Hut to calm her. Thin-crust cheese-and-sausage. But no such luck."

"Our old standby? You're kidding."

"Nope. She said she was a bad person and didn't deserve anything."

"Where in the world did that come from?"

"Who knows? You'd have been proud of me, though. I knelt beside her and said, 'Mom, after all that's gone on today, I think it's time to go to Theda Clark for professional help.' She glared at me like I was the devil."

I knew that look; Mom had perfected it long ago. "You're stronger than you realize, Jude."

"I guess so. In the car Bev praised me for being a good daughter. Mom nearly choked."

A wave of sympathy for my sister rushed over me. Although I was grateful she had Bev, I wished I'd been the one by her side.

"How awful. You're doing all you can." In fact, I'd have done the same. As grown women we often joked about how interchangeable we'd become.

"That's what I told myself," Judy said. "But it gets better. The admitting nurse asked how long Mom's been depressed. I thought *forever* but, of course, I didn't say it out loud. I made it clear, though, that she doesn't go anywhere or see anyone—"

"Or eat, or sleep," I said. "The list is endless." The truth was, she felt life wasn't worth the little she got out of it.

"Well, Mom was so mad, I swore she was going to hit me. 'Who'd be happy living the way I have to? If your dad was alive, he wouldn't believe how you're treating me.'"

"If he was alive, she'd be blaming *him* for her problems."

"Exactly. So, I gave her the bottom line—you, Bill, and I agree her life has to change for the better. God, I did the right thing, didn't I?"

I felt the weight of responsibility shift slightly from Judy's shoulders to mine. "There was nothing else to do."

She sniffed softly. "The main thing is that Mom's safe. I called Bill, too. He warned me not to get my hopes up. He's had patients like her."

"We have to be hopeful. She can't go on like this. Neither can we."

I said good-bye and walked stiffly into the family room, lit only by the TV and Clint Eastwood's *Dirty Harry*. Gary patted the tan leather cushion next to his. I sat down and rested my head on his chest. His warmth relaxed me. Just this once, I didn't mind the robotic gunfire, the bad guys dropping like flies.

3

Judy refolded an eggshell tablecloth, tucked it under its matching napkins in the hutch, and dabbed a thin line of sweat on her upper lip. "You can have Mom's bed tonight."

"I'd prefer the couch," I said, startled by the image of myself staring up at the same ceiling Mom had. I stretched my legs, feeling the damp creases behind my knees, and made a mental note to decipher the air-conditioning system when we stopped for lunch.

"What about the guest room?"

"*I'm* not getting into the bed Dad died in. Besides, that saggy mattress kills my back." Recalling the relative comfort of the living room's brown corduroy couch from previous visits, I knew this night would be different. I'd be surrounded by Mom's life preservers of brass geese on the mantel, watercolor geese in V formation on the wall, and grandmother clock in the corner. With few exceptions, we planned to sell everything.

"Let's ask Bill if he wants the aqua vase he gave Mom."

"And his painting," Judy added wistfully, turning toward our brother's first and only attempt with acrylics, a swirling seascape hanging boldly among the earth tones. I felt an old twinge of jealousy. Judy painted, sculpted, and soldered and polished silver into sparkling bracelets and rings. I'd learned to shun art in any form. Given crayons and blank paper in grade school, I'd produced nothing more than scraggly trees and a sunrise. When a teacher had recommended I not pursue art in the ninth grade after a nonstellar

B minus in the eighth, I'd concluded I didn't have one artistic bone in my body.

I twisted the anniversary band on my finger. "Has he mentioned anything about coming?"

She dropped into the high-backed chair next to mine and undid the second button of her polo. "No, but whatever we decide to do with Mom's stuff is fine by him. Maybe he can't deal with her anymore."

"We do what we can," I said, remembering a pact we'd made: to disprove Mom's theory that one child usually shoulders most of the responsibility for an aging parent. Just as we'd shared our bedroom growing up, Judy and I were bound together by family duty.

I poised my fingers over the keyboard as she stepped into the sunken living room. "Lowboy. Two end tables with leaves. And my personal favorite: round glass table with metal base shaped like harvest wheat."

While I marveled at how all the pieces fit into this average-sized room, my heart ached. Mom would never see or touch her belongings before we'd hand them over to strangers. This was by far the cruelest task—it surpassed our careful selection of the smallest mementos and our upcoming appointments with the attorney and auctioneer.

Judy called the day after Mom's admission to the hospital, her voice trembling like static across the wires. "Mom was rambling incoherently. Her doctor suggested she might be harmful to herself, so he put her in the locked psych ward. Mom begged me to take her home. I told her I couldn't, and she cried. I cried."

I shut my eyes. They felt bloated and heavy, two pools ready to spill. "I'm sorry," I said.

"She wouldn't change out of her nightgown, or shower either. She said, 'I haven't washed my own hair in forty years, and I don't intend to start now!'"

Mom's love affair with the downtown beauty parlor began when she'd been hired at the printing company. For $10, and a tip, she'd reappear not only expertly coiffed but rejuvenated as well.

"I'd had it. I took clean panties from her bag and said, 'It's time for breakfast, so get dressed.'"

"Way to go."

"Well," Judy sighed, "she yanked them on but snapped her legs back under the covers. I was firm. 'Fine. Expect everyone to cater to you, just like Grandma.' If looks could kill, Con, I'd have been plastered to the wall."

I pictured Mom clasping a thin cotton blanket like a child refusing to get up for school. "I'm sorry she's so hard on you."

"Here's the psychiatrist's take—Mom's cruel to me, yet I'm not cruel back because I'm a strong person. These were his exact words to her: 'I bet all three of your children are strong, or they wouldn't have survived in your household.'"

My pulse quickened. It was as if he'd peered through our aluminum windows on State Street.

"Mom yelled, 'I'll have you fired!' Imagine that. Virginia is still up to her old tricks."

As a child, I tried not to get in anyone's way. For the most part, I avoided Bill, secretly wishing for a lock on my bedroom door like my friend Pam had on hers. She played in her room without fearing a brother storming in, tossing her on the floor, and tickling her until she begged for mercy. Yet when Bill or I was sick in bed, we entertained each other as if we'd been grand pals all along. I showed him how to blow bubbles with Bazooka gum, and he taught me to whistle. I marched happily through the house, displaying my newfound talent, fooled into thinking our camaraderie could last.

On rainy or wintry days, I retreated to the cavernous basement, losing myself in the task-oriented rooms of laundry, storage, play, and workshop. Dad had painted the block walls citrine and beige, and the concrete floors sleek ivy and mahogany. I felt like an intruder slinking into his workshop at the left of the landing, yet one pull of a string above my head lit saws hanging on pegboard and nails in baby-food jars. The air was just as irresistible, filled with the scents of his current projects—sandpapered pine for shelves, a coffee cup resurrected with

Elmer's. Sometimes Dad let me hammer, and with the steady chink of metal on metal, I finally ruled a tiny portion of my world.

The main attraction in the basement for my sister and brother was the homemade Ping-Pong table. It seemed like a perfect arrangement, the ball swooshing from one green side to the other while I rooted for the underdog, Judy. That is, until the day they dropped their red paddles, raced from the playroom in different directions, and returned, Bill dragging Grandma C's rocker and Judy brandishing a dish towel from the clothesline. I was stunned when they plopped me onto the seat and wrapped the wet rag around my ribs, yanking its ends through the slats behind me. A large, hard knot kept me securely in place.

"Let me go!" I screamed over and over when they tipped me upside down; I was certain of Mom's appearance with a wooden spoon in hand. She never came. They continued their game of twenty-one while I whimpered like a tiger cub I'd seen at the Milwaukee County Zoo.

It seemed as if hours passed before Mom called, "Supper!" Judy untied the towel and scrambled upstairs beside Bill. She debated her loss, as if that had been the only event of the day. I stomped behind and grudgingly took my place at the table. Looking down at my empty plate, I spewed the humiliating details of my captivity.

"I figured you three were just *playing*," Mom said matter-of-factly, handing the mashed potatoes to Dad. He pointed his knife at the butter dish, his signal to pass it down. And that was that. Being her favorite child hadn't garnered me an ounce of sympathy, not even a hug.

Dad didn't talk much. While he and I silently drove to eleven o'clock Mass, I'd observe him shift gears, his tanned wrist protruding from his starched white cuff like an earthworm startled by daylight. With all my might, I'd try to think of something witty to say but usually failed, relieved we lived only four blocks from St. John's.

I believed all fathers were workers by day, newspaper-readers and TV-watchers by night. On weekends they preferred sports in the comfort of their living rooms. Dad would light a Camel and switch on golf, and I'd join him, especially if handsome Arnold Palmer was playing. He was the most cheerful man I'd ever seen, waving to fans clustered along the lush fairway. When he reached the green and eyed the tiny cup with his putter, the TV announcer reduced his voice to a whisper, the gallery stood silent, and I followed suit. I didn't want to jinx Mr. Palmer.

Although Dad was a man of few words, he wasn't shy about punishing us when he saw fit. One night when I was reading with the TV on, someone changed the channel. Without looking up, I yelled, "Turn that back, stupid!" Before I knew it, Dad had me by the elbow, his other hand planted squarely across my rear. "I thought you were Bill," I said tearfully as he led me to my room. An hour later, when he invited me to sit on his lap for the last bit of evening, I knew I'd been darn lucky.

Bill usually didn't fare as well. I'd feel the floor shake with Dad's purpose, hear Mom ask impatiently, "Now what?" and see Dad storm into Bill's room with his good leather belt. After each slap, I'd tighten my arms around my knees to keep them from shaking. This punishment was Bill's alone, as if his name had been imprinted into the hide with big gold letters. At Sunday Mass I stared at Dad's belt, remembered Bill's defiant face, and prayed for a time when we'd all get along.

After school each day, Judy became more like a referee between Bill and me. From our room, she'd bellow over her music, "Quit fighting!" She never saw what happened after Bill tired of our rubber-band games.

I knew when it was time to run for cover. Bill would toss aside his chair cushion and stand up, eyeing me like a tomcat about to pounce on a robin. I never got far before I felt the strength in his teenage hands. He'd throw me onto the couch and twist my ankles round and round, burning my face on the scratchy fabric. Then he'd grab one wrist and foot, and in an instant I'd be airbound, circling the room faster and faster, until all the golds and olives blurred like our backyard maple. When he'd finally drop me and add some punches into the fleshy part of my arms for good measure, I would silently curse him.

On Saturdays I'd confess to taking the name of God in vain. "The words of sinners," old Father Joe would blast from his side of the mesh curtain, where he considered himself invisible. My penance of five Our Fathers and five Hail Marys seemed like a meager price to pay for Bill's battering.

Yet I was a "sinner"! It confirmed everything the nuns had taught. The brand was hot and sickening. No matter how well-behaved I tried to be, there was always something or someone to fear.

My only recourse was to tattle when Mom came home from work. "*Do not hit your sister!*" she'd scold, clearly enunciating each word. "And, Connie, stop pestering your brother. I can't watch you two every waking minute. There'll be times when you have to fend for yourself."

"But, Mom!" I'd stutter, wanting to say that this wasn't one of them. By then she'd be gone, charging down the hallway to change out of her dress. I was determined to convince her of my innocence. A spattering of bruises wasn't enough.

Showers drenched Northern California the last weekend in April, and early-morning shadows kept me in bed longer than usual. The house was utterly quiet. Gary had taken a week off from our general-contracting business and flown to the Fox River Valley to help his parents remodel. Cara slept in, postponing a book report and an ongoing argument with a girlfriend. Even Jack stretched his warm puppy limbs alongside mine and snored ever so slightly. Although the carpet needed vacuuming and laundry sat in color-coded heaps in the hallway, I sank my face into the pillow. Nothing could block out my mother.

Judy's most recent call played in my head. "The doctor wants to run more tests. He thinks Mom is very confused."

I recalled our family reunion the previous summer. Mom had driven by the designated picnic spot in Jefferson Park even though thirty of us, holding cans of Coke and Miller Lite, had waved to get her attention. She'd gone on home, claiming later "it didn't look familiar." I'd thought she'd simply been stubborn, preferring to be alone over conversing with Rita and Don, Rosemary, and various cousins. Nothing else made sense. Jefferson Park was three blocks from

Grandma C's house. Every Fourth of July we'd ramble down 2nd Street as the sun dropped behind the water tower, scout out an acceptable spot in the sea of blankets, and watch fireworks. Jefferson Park was where Mom and Dad first met.

"And he thinks her physical symptoms are very creative. Of course, she blew a gasket."

"*Finally*, Judy. Someone else is saying it."

"He also talked about Grandma being a hypochondriac."

We'd heard the tale many times: four daughters, a mother ruling the world from her bed while the father worked the Soo Line, and a half-crippled grandmother who cleaned and cooked for all of them in their two-story Victorian on Forest Avenue.

"All in all, he was right on the money," Judy added sadly. "He said, 'Virginia, let's break the cycle of mental illness in your family right now.' Mom looked him straight in the eye and sneered, 'Mister, I'm nothing like my mother.'"

I was five the day of Grandpa's funeral. While aunts washed syrupy breakfast dishes and uncles smoked in the parlor, I stood at the bottom of the staircase, wondering why Grandma hadn't come down. Impatiently, I grabbed the banister and snuck up the stairs. From the top step I saw her, lying down in a black dress, her silver pin curls ringed by patches of pink scalp. Perhaps she'd caught whatever had made Grandpa sick.

Later I learned she spent weeks in bed, alternating with stints in the county mental hospital. I was an adolescent when I saw Winnebago's brick buildings rise like hideous growths against the autumn country-side. Maintaining a safe distance behind Mom, I nearly jumped out of my skin as a buzzer unlocked one door, then another, steel gray and dictionary thick. I instantly regretted my earlier decision to accompany her, when she'd packed dark chocolates into a pumpkin-colored tin and promised our visit would be short.

We hurried down musty hallways. Flat, pasty faces peered through windows on each door, and I shivered. When we found Grandma's room, I swear Mom took the same deep breath I did. Yet in we walked as if we were regulars, handing Grandma the candy, tidying up her nightstand, and commenting on the changing seasons.

She didn't seem any "crazier" than normal, just shrunken and doll-like on a straight-backed chair, her speckled hands folded tightly in her lap. Other than a meek "thank you" before biting into a candy, she didn't speak. Mom's sad eyes locked onto mine, and I understood a daughter's duty. She'd needed me, and I was thankful I hadn't let her down.

"If it's any consolation," I said to Judy, "Gary's close by, and my train arrives Friday." Even though I'd bought the ticket before Mom's hospital admission, my love of train travel, its extravagance of time away from the accounting end of our business, seemed suddenly quite selfish.

"Good, because they're estimating another week. And she's got a roommate. Twenty-one at the most. Attempted suicide. I thought, *Oh, great. If Mom's depressed now* . . . But when her parents visited, Mom chimed right in as if they were old friends."

I was familiar with her splashed-on congeniality. While sunbathing in our backyard on State Street, she'd gossip good-naturedly with the next-door neighbor, who walked from her grass to ours after hanging laundry on her clothesline. When she left, Mom grumbled about how boring she was.

"So later I said, 'How can you sound normal around other people and then make a scene when I'm here?' I told her you and I would be talking guardianship. You should have seen her, Con. Got out of bed, yanked on her jeans, took off down the hallway, yelling, 'I'm stronger than you think!'"

I saw Mom perfectly, her stride quick and resolute, as if on a mission to find a sales clerk in Jandry's.

4

"I'm ready for my afternoon nap," Judy said while unlocking Mom's back door. "I ate too much."

"You're out of luck." I smiled. "Duty calls."

I climbed the step behind her, then turned around. How sad Mom couldn't witness the end of summer: Red primroses spanned a neighbor's driveway, and sunflowers reigned over his garden. Yet she'd probably just complain about her own yard, the color of toast and a hotbed for thistles. It was a far cry from being the pride of the neighborhood, as it had been under her careful supervision and Dad's green thumb.

"Which bedroom should we tackle?" I asked, shutting the door to the sweltering heat. Before she answered, I took my laptop from the table and headed for the guest room. I'd put off the master for as long as possible.

The walnut dressers were the only pieces of furniture to have survived the rummage sale on State Street. A portable TV sat in the center of the long, narrow one. After Dad passed away, Mom napped regularly on the paisley-quilted bed, and I'd persuaded her to move the TV from the kitchen. Little did I know the amount of time she'd spend in this room.

Judy pulled out the drawers and fell back on her heels. Hidden under layers of tissue paper were lavender sachets, Christmas candles and ornaments, spools of ribbon, Hallmark cards, and birthday gifts in their original boxes.

"I was wondering what became of these wind chimes," Judy said, untangling geometric shapes knotted by thin wire. "I gave them to her at least three summers ago."

"Maybe she couldn't decide where to hang them," I offered. I pictured Mom tucking them into the back of the bottom drawer and muttering, "What's the point? I'm going to die soon anyway."

Gary called around noon on the day before my departure on Amtrak.

"I just talked to Don. Theda Clark is releasing your mom! Someone has to pick her up. He can't—car's in the shop. I guess I'll have to."

"What the hell? How can they release her?"

"Something about no psychiatric grounds. Being a nasty, cantankerous old woman isn't enough. And she isn't suicidal. Do I take her home?"

"What else can we do? It's a big mistake." I wanted to add my trip by train was, too, but I kept my second-guessing to myself. Gary had already come by far more than he'd bargained for.

I stumbled through the rest of my packing, recalling how I'd boarded the California Zephyr to the Midwest for the first time after Dad was diagnosed with cancer. "You're taking the *train?*" Mom had asked incredulously. I'd had vertigo for eight months after a flight from Bill's. I wasn't ready to risk it.

Without a sleeping berth, I'd carefully scanned the coach car for a seatmate whom I wouldn't mind chatting with by day or possibly leaning against at night. Mary was a grandmother from Oakland who toured the country seasonally to be with her children. She looked ready for a family picnic in comfortable black pumps and an ivory shawl hung loosely over her dark skin. She'd claimed her aisle seat with an air of experience. Magazines, Ziploc bags of dried fruit, pastel yarns, and knitting needles filled a canvas tote on the floor. I climbed confidently into the window seat beside her. "Going all the way to New York," she began by way of introduction. "Seventy-five years old and still hop from town to town with no one stopping me." Before we even crossed the state line, I knew I'd made a fine choice.

The hours of chatting, reading, and snoozing were uplifting. As the train snaked through Blue Canyon, over the ripples of Nevada, and across rust-colored Utah, I thought I'd never need to fly again. When the sun went down, Mary stood her shoes next to the tote, placed her shawl squarely over her lap, and wished me a good night's sleep. I took it without hesitation.

"Your mom refused to sign the release papers," Gary steamed while I zipped my suitcase. "They let me take her home anyway."

"What are they thinking?" I shot back. "She needs help right now!"

"I told her I'd sleep here tonight, after I finish Dad's drywall. She begged me not to leave. Maybe you should put her on a plane to our house, or maybe Judy should take her." Then he whispered, "Just so you know, I put her pills and car keys on top of the cupboard above the stove. I'm not taking any chances."

"Thank you," I said. "I appreciate it immensely."

I pictured Mom's key ring lying beside a multitude of stubby brown bottles. She was the one who always wanted to be the keeper of the keys, the guard over all our lives. I wished I were there to reassure her. I understood a thing or two about fear.

"Where the hell have you been?" Mom screamed. "You left two hours ago to take them home! I suppose they opened the liquor cabinet and you had a merry little Christmas."

I thought I'd been dreaming as I rolled over. Then it hit—it was Christmas Eve.

Grandma and Florian had joined us, as they did every year. We stuffed ourselves with ham and apple pie and exchanged presents under the tree. Afterward, the grown-ups retreated to the kitchen. Mom served Folgers in Candlewick cups, and they played fast rounds of poker for real money. I circled behind them, careful not to give away anyone's hand by giggling or raising my eyebrows. When they tired of the game, they moved on to cribbage, keeping score with pegs on the board Dad made. By ten o'clock, everyone claimed exhaustion. Grandma and Florian kissed us kids on the forehead, and Dad drove them home.

"It's all in your head, Virginia." His words swirled in the air like headlines in the *Twin City News*. "I only had a couple of drinks, so stop griping."

I jumped over to Judy's bed by the wall. She raised the covers, and I burrowed into the folds of her red flannel nightgown.

"Well, your brother certainly lives the carefree life. No responsibilities. No children. Still living with his mother. Don't think you're like him, because you're not!"

As Dad stomped toward the living room, I wondered if sometimes we were all too much for him. A universe jammed with gangly kids and backyard chores. Even though Mom was angry at him, why ridicule Florian? He had a fine life as the tender of the town's Main Street Bridge, manning it every day except in winter when the Fox River froze. I envied him, sitting high above the world in the small brick box. When the weather turned hot, he perched on the concrete stoop in a sleeveless white T-shirt and tuned his transistor radio to the Braves game. He waved his cocoa-colored arms at passing drivers as if they were all long-lost friends.

When Judy and I walked downtown to the library on Saturday mornings, we visited Florian on the way. He'd point excitedly toward the docks. "See that beauty?" He was all motion then, jerking levers and pressing fist-sized buttons as if he were playing pinball. Signals flashed and crossing guards dropped. He turned a large steering wheel round and round, and the bridge split in two. As the yacht puttered beneath the giant gray V, he'd say, "Aren't they lucky?"

In his free time, Florian pedaled his black Schwinn to our house. "Hey, Gin!" he'd bellow over the slam of the screen door. Mom would roll her eyes and continue peeling potatoes with emphatic flicks of her wrist. When he sang "Constantinople," I scrambled into his big bear hug before the last syllable left his lips.

Florian sat on the step stool in a kitchen corner and told stories about his army days in France. Instead of battles, he bragged of being a businessman, trading food and, surprisingly, his boots for cigarettes. Then he'd retrieve two Alka-Seltzer tablets from a cupboard, stir them in lukewarm water, and swallow the mixture like it was cream soda. Mom bristled. Yet, since no one else used the antacid, I wondered if she'd had a soft spot for him after all. It was probably more likely that she wanted his stomach to settle so he'd go home. She'd say, "Anyone that age living with his mother and glued to a barstool gets what he deserves."

I plopped onto my bulging suitcase and dialed my in-laws.

"Hello!" someone said lightheartedly after one ring.

"Who's this?" I asked, forgetting to identify myself.

"I'm the plumber. Here, let me grab one of 'em for ya."

Luckily for me, Gary came on the line. "Hey. Your mom's here, but everything's under control."

"What's she doing there?"

"Actually, she's sitting on a folding chair in the middle of the hall-way," he said. "She didn't want to be alone, so I brought her over. She's watching me patch the bedroom ceiling."

"So, Mom's really *not* okay if she's—"

"Con, she keeps asking when you and Judy are coming. I'll put her on."

I nibbled on my fingernails. I wasn't sure when I'd acquired the habit.

"Hi, Connie," Mom said breathlessly, as if she'd been exercising. "Gary was nice enough to let me come over, but I don't think the rest of them care for me. I'll just stay a few more minutes."

"That sounds like the right thing to do."

"Connie, did you know that when Judy took me to the hospital the other night, there was a terrible storm?"

My chest tightened. "Mom, listen to me."

"I am! Well, it reminded me of how I almost died in the Peshtigo fire."

She was mistaken; her grandmother was the one who'd been saved. "Mom, you need to help yourself, right now. Do you want me to think you're crazy? When I get there . . . "

"Oh, thank God you're coming."

After we hung up, I thought about the next few days. There would be hundreds of miles of desert and grassland to brace myself for the words *incompetence* and *guardianship*. Yet I wasn't sure I was up to the task. I'd have to look her in the eye and tell the truth—that her behavior was far from normal and things had to change. Including me. I'd need to summon as much courage as possible.

The following morning, I shoved my suitcase into the luggage bin on the Zephyr's lower level, then climbed the tenuous steps to coach. With only a limited number of empty seats, I chose one alongside a beefy, middle-aged man already slumped against a window. I tried not to visualize our nighttime positions.

My mind constantly wandered back to Mom. Reading didn't help. Gazing out the curved windows of the observation car was worse. Boxcars advertised the Virginia Railroad in white block letters. Road signs pointed south to Virginia City. There was no escaping the word of the day.

When the train pulled into Denver Thursday afternoon, I checked my cell phone for messages. One missed call from Judy. My stomach lurched. I played the scene Judy had outlined repeatedly in my head as we rumbled through Nebraska and crossed the Mississippi. Mom had called 911 again, and a policeman had driven her to the hospital. As Iowa fields whizzed by, I pictured Mom rinsing sweet corn in the kitchen sink, her fingers covered in silky strands. Then I saw them again, anxiously fluttering against the sleeve of a patient young man who helped her into his patrol car. This time, the hospital would have to keep her. She was finally safe.

"I'm here," I said, kissing Mom's papery cheek. She turned slowly on a gray plastic chair and faced me. I'd never seen eyes like hers before— flat as soapstone, charred pinpoints pasted dead center. She lowered her head to the folding table, and I noticed her unbrushed hair, the abundance of dandruff across her navy shoulders. I sank into a chair next to her, thankful I'd skipped breakfast.

"I left Wednesday on Amtrak," I began, as if she was listening.

The sole response came from a young woman slouched at the far end of the room. "Took a train once with my daddy," she said. Strings of fraying gauze from a bandaged wrist snipped the air as she covered her ears and groaned, "Noise, day and night. Didn't get a minute of sleep."

Her eyes were almost turquoise. They twitched and blinked with such regularity that I thought it would be unbearable, the continuous motion, the bleeding out, then in, of light. I saw myself as a small girl, standing in my closet with the door shut, careful not to disturb the cotton blouses Mom had pressed. With one swift pull of the light chain above me, my favorite blues and greens came to life. With another equally swift yank, the light dissolved, and with it all the magnificent color.

If I hadn't known better, I would have thought Mom was sleeping, her fingers splayed now beneath her cheek. She didn't move when Judy joined us at the table.

"Mom's not eating today," she reported.

I touched Mom's free hand. Her normally clear-polished nails were bare and jagged. As I wondered if she'd stopped using her Jergens, she raised her head and sneered, "The food is *crap*. Slop fit for pigs." Her eyes pierced mine, and I knew in that moment she hated me. Of course, she hated Judy, too, for leaving her in this place. I was struck by a new wave of nausea.

I'd seen the look of hatred before in my mother's eyes: her owl-like stare out the kitchen window, waiting for Dad to stumble up the driveway after beers and shots at Tony's, on paydays when he came home a few dollars short. One night, after supper dishes had been dried and homework checked, Mom saw Dad slumped against the snowy hood of our car. She screeched out the back door, "Get in this goddamn house right now!"

He grinned lopsidedly. Mom then turned abruptly toward Judy and hissed, "You have your dad wrapped around your little finger. You bring him in!"

Judy looked as if she'd been stung, shades of pink consuming her cheeks. She quickly did as she was told. I thought she was fearless crouched beside Dad, moving her lips. When he raised his arms and shooed her away, she limped into the house with her chin stuck to her chest.

Only a minute passed before Dad appeared, dangling on the

landing while judging the distance between his right foot and the step up into the kitchen.

"You idiot!" Mom yelled.

"Shut up, Virginia. Just go to hell."

The "h"-word seemed to drip from his mouth. Judy grabbed my hand, and we ran to our bedroom. We tumbled into the dark closet and huddled on the cold wood floor. From the other side of the wall, I heard slaps of flesh on flesh. I imagined Dad sprawled across their bed, too weak to fight back. "Virginia, don't leave," he moaned after a door slammed.

I cried into Judy's shoulder. Her cheek brushed mine, and I realized she was crying, too.

"He laughed at me," she said.

I was certain I'd never be as brave.

When we said good-bye to Mom at the hospital, I left behind a part of me, the girl who had curled up beside her during *Lawrence Welk* and caressed her creamy skin. I could hardly bear to leave her alone otherwise. The charge nurse displayed little warmth; I disliked her yet envied her detachment at the same time. However, I also felt closer to my mother than I ever had. It was my turn to honor and guard the intimate details of her life.

"Mom's determined to be sick," Judy said, maneuvering her Taurus through the late-afternoon traffic back to the Palisades. We passed Corr Opticians on the corner of Commercial Street and Forest Avenue, where Mom's childhood home had been razed and replaced by a concrete building adorned with two beady eyeballs framed in red neon.

"It's different this time, isn't it?" I asked. "Something's going on in her head."

"Well, all I'm saying is Mom's a manipulator, pure and simple. If she can't get her way, look out."

Mom's refusal to eat lunch could have been manipulation, especially since she had no problem with the carrot cake. Everything else, her slovenly appearance and unresponsiveness, spoke of more than an old woman trying to get attention. I sank into the worn upholstery, anxious about tomorrow's MRI and psychological evaluation. Yet, armed with medical evidence and opinions, I was hopeful we'd figure it out. Every ounce of love for my mother would make sure of it.

5

As we hugged good night, I felt Judy tremble with exhaustion from the long day at the psych ward. I was reluctant to let her go. Any squeamish feelings I'd had regarding hospitals and sickness had been erased years ago. I'd been the careless, clumsy child: falling from monkey bars, scraping the skin off my right cheek; riding my bike into a telephone pole, breaking my nose; stepping on a broken pop bottle, almost slicing the artery in my left ankle. And a three-week hospital stay due to kidney disease, followed by six months of home care, had eased the trauma of bedpans, needles, and X-ray machines with multiple squid-like limbs.

I tucked a sheet into the sofa cushions and lay on my side, facing the window. Through the sheers I traced the outline of the moon and wondered where it hung in my part of the world. Then I saw myself driving up my street as a quarter moon appeared above the roof lines. Had Mom found comfort in the beauty of the nighttime sky? Had she taken the time to look?

I knew something was wrong the moment I sat down to breakfast one August morning before the start of third grade.

"What's the matter with your neck?" Mom asked, handing me a plate of buttermilk pancakes.

I was confused by her question, since only minutes separated my waking and stumbling to the chair. She lifted my bangs and felt my forehead. Her penciled brows shot up like rockets.

"My God, you're hot! Judy, flip the pancakes. I'm calling the doctor."

My sister eyed me appreciatively. She was momentarily in charge, a rare event in our mother's kitchen. I, on the other hand, was terrified by Mom's reaction, even more so when I realized that my face hurt: cheeks, chin, the bumpy ridge of my jaw. The skin on my twisted neck was like a rubber band stretched to its limit.

"We're meeting him at the hospital, Connie," Mom said while hurrying to her bedroom. From the closet shelf she retrieved a tweed suitcase. Her voice softened. "There's nothing to cry about. Janice was a whole year younger than you when she had her tonsils out. She didn't cry."

As Mom packed my summer pajamas, I doubted everything she said about Janice.

At Theda Clark I was given my own room on the fourth floor. In the dreary, cave-like space, nurses propped thermometers under my tongue and placed cold stethoscopes on my chest. I couldn't imagine what was wrong and desperately wished for somewhere to hide. I pictured myself crouched beside the creek bed just past 9th Street. It was a sanctuary for turtles. They'd leisurely climb the smooth rocks, sunbathe for a while, and then slink into the dull brown water when the heat got the best of them.

The loneliness was overwhelming. How strange to lie in a bed without my sister in a matching one next to me. We had always shared our yellow bedroom: half a dresser, half a closet. There was no one here to whisper to in the dark. No one, as it turned out, who believed that enormous spiders crawled through the air conditioner onto the wall by the foot of my bed once the lights were switched off. Judy never would have said, "You're seeing things, honey," like the grouchy night nurse did.

On the second day, Dr. Jensen told us that I had nephritis, an infection deep within my kidneys. "After we get it under control, she'll need months of bed rest." I sobbed into my pillow with the slight strength I had.

It hurt to move. Each morning I lay quietly on my back, hunting for shapes in the swirling patterns of the ceiling tile. I stared at the wall clock and waited for the cleaning lady to arrive. She was the grandmother of fraternal twins in my class; her lips were the color of raspberries, her cheeks powdered and rouged. She'd heave a string mop from a pail to the floor, smile between slaps of ammonia, and chirp, "You'll be out of here in no time." I wasn't so sure.

Mom came an hour or so later, flinging open the drapes and straightening my tangled sheets. Her routine wasn't all that different from the one at home; however, now she dreamily brushed my waist-length hair. I felt like Rapunzel, posed on top of a tower for all the world to see. Yet, after Mom divided the blond mass into two equal parts and braided them into orderly subjects, it was only *my* reflection in her oval hand mirror.

She also brought mail: colorful get-well cards from relatives, notes on tablet paper from classmates, and, most important, letters from my brother and sister. They reported neighborhood news and pasted the comic strip *Nancy* on pastel stationery. Judy was also my accountant, totaling the unused grape jellies and salt and peppers that Mom took home from my meal trays. They even sent away for the Little Miss Kay doll I'd wanted ever since I'd seen her on a Rice Krispies box, wearing a ruby dress and lace pinafore. The day she arrived was glorious—I finally had another roommate.

Dad visited every afternoon. He never tired of playing War, laying card after card with childish enthusiasm. I felt special not having to compete with anyone for his attention. He made me laugh when I didn't think I could.

After two weeks I was transferred to the children's ward, a bright L-shaped room lined with narrow beds. A chubby girl in the one next to mine occupied herself with a poster set of farm animals and let me be Connie, the dairy cow, while she was the adorable chicken. She clucked and I mooed unhappily, preferring to whinny like the capable plow horse. As the days passed, she seemed less eager to play. When I woke one morning, the girl and her animals were gone. A nurse said she'd been moved to a private room. I hoped *she* wasn't afraid of spiders.

Judy and I secluded ourselves in Mom's house over the weekend in between quick trips to the psych ward. As we cracked windows and breathed invigorating spring air, I could almost hear Mom's lecture on pollen and other offensive substances, and my usual retort: "Fresh air is not your enemy."

Judy tapped my arm and pointed to the basement steps. "Let's start with her strongbox. We know she's not coming home."

Startled by her admission, I followed. Why Mom spent half of her life in an underground family room was beyond me. Although furnished with Ethan Allen and her pewter collection, it smelled like every musty basement I'd ever been in. Even though the taupe carpet appeared brand new, having replaced an orange shag flooded during a thunderstorm, it felt damp under my bare feet.

An RCA console hugged the right wall. Facing it was a seating arrangement that had never changed: olive chair and matching plaid love seat, walnut rocker with an orange paisley cushion. I pictured Mom, paging through *Redbook* on the love seat, while Dad rocked Miffy, the Siamese cat they'd adopted from Bill after one of his moves. Miffy was treated like a member of the family, only his supple feet were more adaptable to their quiet existence. I wanted to be loved that way, cared for as if I'd die tomorrow.

I felt like I was breaking and entering when I turned the door-knob to the unfinished portion of the basement. Dad's Craftsman tool chest, now holding Mom's important papers, glinted in a beam of light on the workbench. Judy raised the lid. Neatly bound with rubber bands were bank statements, life insurance policies, their birth certificates and marriage license, and, at the very bottom, Dad's death certificate.

If Mom could have had her way, her final accounting would have been filed here, too. Born in October 1923, married the day after Christmas twenty-one years later, widowed in 1993. *Misery might be applicable for cause of death,* I thought, feeling a sudden twinge of guilt. Spying into her private life and cynical as well—my sins were adding up faster than I could count them.

Judy dragged the box into the family room and sat beside it.

"Give me a minute," I said. I went back upstairs, grateful for daylight. How I missed seeing Mom here, dusting tables, arranging knickknacks. I leaned on a counter and cried.

"The psychiatrist has declared your mother incompetent," a woman said into the phone the next morning. Even though I expected this pronouncement, the words hit hard. *Malnourished. Dehydrated. Determined to die.* "He'd like to meet with you and your sister."

I made the appointment and relayed the message to Judy.

"How are we going to get through the rest of this day?" she asked, touching my shoulder after I placed the wall phone onto its receiver.

"I don't know. Let's get out of here. Eat, go for a drive, act like normal people."

For several hours we rode around the town where we'd grown up. Past the high school, then St. John's. "There's the convent," Judy said, almost holding her breath. "I had to ring the bell once. . . . "

I glanced at her and we laughed. But I remembered Saturday afternoons in the church basement when I was in fifth grade. Scraping candle wax off glass votives. Scrubbing them clean in a deep metal sink filled with hot water. Waiting for Sister to inspect each one.

From Main Street we drove to Mihm's, the hangout after winter Blue Inn dances and summer ones in Smith Park. Once again we sat on chrome stools and ordered chocolate malts. In an odd way it felt as though I'd never lived in any other place.

Before heading back to the Palisades, Judy turned down State Street and parked the station wagon in front of our old next-door neighbor's house. As we stepped onto the sidewalk, a tall, befuddled man came out of his garage and asked, "Judy?" It was little Dennis, all grown up, of course, and I was amazed at how his thick bangs still hid his high forehead. After explaining that he'd bought the house from his mother, he said the neighbor wasn't home and probably wouldn't mind if we had a look.

My head spun as we walked on the spongy grass beneath the living-room window, then that of our bedroom. They seemed so close together, as if air and space had been squeezed from the structure with the passing of time. The screens I'd once stared out of were clouded with dust. I pictured Dad hosing them off and leaning the silver mesh against the front juniper bushes to dry.

And I thought he'd have marveled at the peach trees he'd planted the summer before my senior year. They dwarfed the backyard; his garden was a vague dirt outline in their shade. Gone, too, was the open spot where Mom sunbathed. I wondered if she'd ever driven by the house after Dad died.

I could barely look into the screened porch off the garage, but I did. Every spring Dad had painted the walls and concrete floor in beiges and greens, like those in our basement. He spent his evenings here under the glow of a floor lamp, with a book propped on his lap and a pipe in his mouth. Thirty years later, I could still smell fresh paint and the scent of his favorite tobacco.

Now the porch was drab and unswept. Patio furniture and toys were stored in haphazard abandon. I was sure my parents would shake their heads in disgust.

"I spoke to your mother," the psychiatrist said that afternoon, peering over bifocals roosting on the tip of his prominent nose. "She's aware that her tests detected dementia-type Alzheimer's."

I quickly turned my head toward Mom, sunk between Judy and me on a too-soft sofa. She stared at nothing in particular, and her shoulders drooped as if she'd been hung on a clothesline to dry. I patted her hand, noticing the age spots she'd always detested.

He showed us the MRI with the obvious dissolution of gray matter. Then he picked up her chart and continued. "Virginia failed virtually every level of memory, typical of storage deficits associated with Alzheimer's. One task, for example, was to draw the face of a clock. She positioned the hours backward." He looked up. "Her life can improve with a sensible diet and medicine. She'll need guidance. A social worker will recommend a suitable living arrangement. Virginia, you can leave here in a couple of days."

Mom didn't respond, and we hardly did either. I was shocked to think that a disease was partially to blame for her bitter relentlessness, and even grateful this was so. However, reality zeroed in. By the end of the week, we'd have Mom packed and moved. I held her hand tightly in mine. I didn't want to let go. Not now. Not ever.

I was released from the hospital and allowed to go home during the second week of September. As Dad pulled the Valiant into our driveway, I spotted Pam standing by the garage, motionless, as if playing statue. Her wide eyes caught mine and I smiled; she quickly turned and ran through the backyard. I was disappointed by the welcome but satisfied with the certainty of her spreading the news.

In the room I shared with my sister, Mom tucked me under cool sheets and gave instructions to Judy and Bill. "Now, remember, Connie is very sick. Don't run in the hallway. Tap lightly on her door." Mom followed Dr. Jensen's orders religiously: fluids, bed rest, limited company, and weekly blood draws by a visiting nurse.

Everyone whispered in the tomblike house. Although I felt like a freak, I secretly loved the safe haven I shared with Little Miss Kay. Somehow it even seemed like a reward for the humiliations of being the youngest. For the first month I rested or slept until Judy and Bill returned from school. Judy hung up her A-line skirt, pulled on black stretch pants, and bragged about eighth grade. One day she and her girlfriends broke the rules and stayed in their classroom during lunch. When they heard Sister Agnella's beads clacking down the hallway, Judy hid in a coat closet while the others crawled out a window and climbed onto the roof. Even though they'd been punished, I was envious of Judy's growing world. I wondered if I'd ever catch up.

By October I was stronger and able to sit up in bed. My tutor, Mrs. Mason, came every morning for arithmetic, science, and spelling lessons. A neighbor woman from down the street brought a lemon tree. She explained how the roots of the six-inch plant would strengthen over winter so it could be planted outside in spring. Unfortunately, it wilted within weeks and dropped all its leaves.

On Halloween morning Mom gave me my first store-bought costume: a suede Indian-princess skirt and vest, trimmed with turquoise beads and fringe. "Try it on," she said.

Puzzled, I slid to the edge of the bed. "I can't trick-or-treat."

"Just for fun," she insisted, holding out the skirt.

I shrugged and stood slowly, my legs thin and as limp as Silly Putty. Mom steadied me, then zipped and buttoned until my transformation was complete. Before I knew it, we were shuffling to the kitchen, where Bill waited with a goofy smile on his face.

"Wanna know why we have all these cupcakes?" he asked, pointing to dozens of orange and white–frosted beauties.

"Don't give it away!" Mom yelled.

It was too late—I heard the slamming of car doors. From the window I saw parents and classmates I hadn't laid eyes on since the end of second grade. They lined up on the sidewalk where I'd roller-skated the night before my ride to the hospital. Leaning against the open front door, I envied them for being on the outside looking in.

A new boy with thick brown glasses sat on a stool and played a concertina. He never took his eyes off me; my cheeks burned as if I'd been centered in a spotlight. When he finished, everyone marched single file to the porch. My hands shook as I silently gave out cupcakes, embarrassed to be the lone person in a costume. I wondered what they'd been told about me. I wanted them to hear everything, especially how before this very moment I had been allowed out of bed only to use the bathroom.

As the holidays approached, my body began to return to life. I watched Mom decorate the tree in the living room with new blue lights and bulbs. After she gave her final approval, she said, "Sit by it and I'll take your picture." I relished the rare occasion and arranged my braids on my daisy-quilted bathrobe. After one flash of the Polaroid, I headed back to my room.

In February I timidly entered St. John's third-grade class. Amid a sprinkling of coughs and sputtering of radiators, Mrs. Prange led me to an empty desk. I felt like a stranger in my too-small wool sweater, its fat yellow collar high on my neck and its wood buttons pressing against my stomach. I had points taken away from me before I even sat down.

"We're drawing landscapes today, Connie. You can use these colored pencils."

I stared a long time at the white construction paper, fearful of failing my first assignment. My fingers carefully shaped the emerald hills I'd seen on *The Wide World of Disney*. I drew broad, leafy trees between them and a lemon half-circle sun on the horizon. Each pencil stroke was crisp and intentional as I created the perfect day. I'd be safe here. I'd never get sick or be embarrassed at school. I'd never hear my parents fight or feel my brother's hands on my body. I would lie on the plush grass and smell the promise of spring. As far as I knew, hope wasn't a sin.

The elder-care attorney was running late for our three o'clock appointment. After nervously scanning his framed licenses on the wall, I considered the money he'd spent refurbishing the ancient house into a modern law office. A massive oak desk and cushioned chairs filled most of the space. I realized that although my father-in-law had recommended Craig, we didn't know his hourly rate.

"Where is he?" Judy whispered. "I want to get this over with."

"Me too. It's so damn quiet I feel like I'm in church."

Actually, I hadn't stepped into one for years. More recently I'd concluded organized religion was big business at the expense of the faithful. The Bible verse "God has not given us the spirit of fear . . . but of a sound mind," seemed as believable as the tooth fairy leaving coins under a child's pillow.

Craig blew into the office in a double-breasted suit. With a flurry of words, he apologized for keeping us waiting. "Court day. Judge was definitely not in a hurry. I've already spoken with the doctor, the social worker, and your brother. He verified everything we've already discussed. We can proceed with temporary guardianship."

"Temporary?" Judy asked. "How long does it last?"

"Sixty days. However, because your mother has been declared incompetent, she can't sign herself into a facility. Temporary guardianship gives you that power. Who will be her guardian?"

Judy and I looked at each other. "Me," she said hesitantly. "We thought Mom could live by Connie."

"Things get quite complicated if a parent doesn't live near the guardian. Care requires on-the-spot decisions, signatures. Since the court system here is fairly clogged, I'd recommend having her protectively placed in Illinois. After that, probate court will require permanent guardianship, which I can coordinate with your attorney there."

I bit the remaining fingernail on my left hand. "Maybe Mom should live by you, Judy."

Instantly, her face turned a dark rose and I knew I'd betrayed her. But even if I could have plucked the horrible words out of the air, I wouldn't have. Gary and I had more than enough to handle at home. Ryan would start his third year of college in the fall. When he had been a freshman, colitis had hit his digestive tract hard. By Thanksgiving he'd lost twenty pounds from his already-slender frame. Now I was anxious about another flare-up. And at sixteen, Cara would balance an independent-study program with ice-skating practices early every morning. The competition season meant a renewed push for consistent jumps, and I feared a reoccurrence of a previous injury—a fractured vertebra from falling on a double axel.

"Well," Judy answered somewhat reluctantly, "I suppose a move to Illinois would be easier than California."

I nodded and tucked my fingers under my thighs. I felt drained.

"It might be a better placement," Craig offered. "Discuss it between you while I check on tomorrow's calendar."

By seven, we returned to the hospital for family night in the psych ward. Rita and Don agreed to join us. When I saw my aunt's short, rotund frame under the yellowish light of the main entrance, I breathed more easily. Rita had always been cheerful; I could confide in her when I needed to. Now she smiled reassuringly and said, "It's just another visit, girls."

I wanted nothing more than to accept her understatement as optimism, to buy a vase of carnations in the gift shop and present it to a mother who'd be grateful to see me. But I knew Mom's anger would make that impossible. I sluggishly followed Rita, Don, and Judy into the elevator.

"It seems I'll be moving Mom by me," Judy said in a low voice after the door closed. She was uncomfortable in confined spaces and hunched into the far corner. "I signed the papers this afternoon."

Rita sighed. "It's for the best. Then we won't have to worry about what's going to happen next. What a shame. Ginny loves her home, her things." She reached for Don's arm as the fourth-floor button beamed red.

I could hardly look at Judy. Ever since we'd left the attorney's office, I had been apprehensive about our decision. What if I'd spoken too soon at Judy's expense? What if she didn't really want to be Mom's guardian? Even though I'd overcome my childhood fear of speaking my mind, I dreaded her disapproval.

The elevator door opened, and I thought perhaps family night had been canceled.

Except for an aide sipping coffee from a paper cup at the nurses' station, there was no one. He stuck out the thick pinkie of his raised hand and pointed down the hall. Mom was sitting alone at a table with her back to us. I could have sworn she hadn't moved all day.

Nonchalantly, Rita pulled out a folding chair across from her. "So, Ginny, what's for supper?"

A tray with a plate of soggy rice and a dryish cut of meat teetered on the edge of the table. I pushed it back to the center and offered Mom a spoonful of the obligatory lime Jell-O. Her eyes bulged in my direction. Creases, resembling furrows of freshly raked sand, settled into her forehead.

"Well, your grandmother's appetite was nonexistent, too," Rita continued good-naturedly. "For years that woman was nothing more than skin."

I pictured Grandma's meticulously powdered face. Even given its current neglect, Mom's was equally flawless and younger-looking than her age suggested.

"*I'm* not touching this garbage," Mom suddenly snarled. As she dropped her head onto her arm, I noticed the frayed sleeve of her T-shirt and made a mental note to shop for new ones. She rarely sorted through her wardrobe; replacing even the most insignificant item proved too distressing. Yet I remembered how effortlessly Mom had discarded my old clothes. Rita would stop by on a Saturday morning and eagerly finger the nightgowns and sweaters folded neatly on the kitchen counter. "My girls will die for these," she'd say while packing them all into brown grocery bags. After she left, Mom would tidy the kitchen and say, "Thank God that's done. At least they'll have some decent things to wear."

Mom made me feel like we had our place in the world: several steps above Rita, about even with Rosemary, and grudgingly behind her third sister, Pat, who'd married an artist and lived in a sprawling house fifteen miles away. Needless to say, we rarely saw Pat, Joe, and my two cousins.

"You know, Cindy was *murdered*," Mom said abruptly. "Yet here they sit, so calm."

I felt as though I'd been punched. How could she say something that heartless in front of my aunt and uncle? Even though seven years had passed since they'd lost their daughter, I was certain the horror would never die. Don's eyes twitched more rapidly than normal. Rita's narrow lips sagged. No one should experience such grief.

Now all heads turned toward a bowlegged man in a doorway, wearing a pin-striped shirt over Depends. Although unshaven, his face looked youthful and serene. As he shuffled in our direction, the aide gently turned him around. Mom shook her head in disbelief and mumbled, "I don't belong here." I was certain she did.

Judy parked her car in Mom's driveway, and neither of us moved to get out. I was amazed at how beautiful Mom's world was. Strands of streetlight filtered through the dense pines of her corner lot. A row of a dozen poplars, rising twenty feet into the blackened sky, separated her backyard from a neighbor's. If it hadn't been for their brightly lit kitchen window, I'd have thought we were on a country road instead of a suburban street.

"Mom looked so bad," I finally said, pulling my jean jacket together. The car cooled quickly, and my breath formed a faint cloud. "Can you believe she's locked up in that place? She should be here, demanding to know why we're late and making us grilled-cheese sandwiches." I laughed at myself, a younger version of Mom yet without her biting tone.

"I didn't know what to say to her," Judy answered. "I usually shut down when she got in a foul mood, and it's no different now." She brusquely took her keys out of the ignition. I slowly opened my door.

Although the landscape was in the throes of spring, the air was chilled and saturated with smoldering firewood. I longed for it to clear my head. As we followed the curved walk to the front porch, I was thankful I'd left the light on. Mom had always been reluctant to do so. A "bug magnet," she'd complained, especially for the annoying mosquito.

I recalled an August visit. Judy and I had made reservations at a hotel with a pool, while Bill planned to stay with Mom. We'd met at O'Hare on a Friday night and driven three sweltering hours north to the Fox Valley. The kids had begged for a swim. We agreed it would be a much-needed break for all of us.

Leaving Bill to lifeguard, Judy and I hurried to my room and called Mom. "Hi, we're here," Judy said into the phone as I sat across from her on one of the double beds. "Ryan and Cara are in the pool."

"Why the hell didn't you call me?" Mom was shouting, and I could hear the exasperation in her voice.

Judy stammered, "I'm doing it now."

I was stunned and motioned for the phone. She handed it over; her knuckles were almost white.

"How can you talk to Judy that way?" I asked.

"Nobody thinks about me. Tell Bill not to come. I'm turning off the light and going to bed."

The dial tone buzzed in my ear. While Judy unlocked Mom's door now, I recalled how Bill had shared Judy's hotel room that vacation, since he hadn't planned on the expense. I realized it was the first time I'd noticed a change in Mom's personality. She hadn't yelled at us with such contempt since we were kids. Her unreasonableness had been more than puzzling. Now it flashed like a beacon, a "Look Out Ahead" warning sign. If only I'd recognized it then. If only it hadn't been another quick spurt of grease in an already-sizzling pan.

Mom's bedroom was awash with sunlight the second morning of our inventory. The brass bed gleamed, its flowered spread smooth and undisturbed. We'd been taught proper bed-making early on: sheets creased at the corners, then tucked beneath the mattress; pillows plumped under the blankets, not over. Bill was the master bed-maker, when he cared to be. Judy was average. My pitiful efforts were usually overlooked, since I was the youngest. Yet I strategically placed baby dolls on the yellow chenille to hide any imperfections.

I picked up two brown teddy bears from the rocker and sat down with my laptop. They'd been gifts from me to soften Mom's formal home, their pastel ribbons gentle reminders of other colors besides the decorator hues of beige and gold. As if they were new members of the family, Mom had positioned them on the sage velveteen cushion from which they never budged. Practically everything had been displayed and untouched for years.

The dusty dresser held a wedding photo of my grandparents, a black-and-white five-by-seven in an antique frame. In Grandma's eyes I caught Mom's consternation, a detachment and lack of merriment that seemed to thrive on her side of the family. Glancing into a mirror, I hoped my own dour image would soon fade.

A seldom-used brass comb-and-brush set rested alongside the photo. When Florian had given it to Mom one Christmas, I considered it extravagant and extremely personal. Now I wondered what it meant to her, if she'd felt an emotional attachment to my favorite uncle. After all, Mom had always maintained her civility toward him even though she'd criticized his drunken ways. I was still doubtful, however, that she'd had the capacity to connect with anyone.

Judy opened the drawers, one after the other. "Not much here. What *did* she wear?"

"Hopefully not this," I groaned, holding up a stretched-out bra that clearly had been laundered too many times. "I'd take her shopping and ask, 'What do you need?' 'Nothing,' she'd say." I laid the bra by the other unattractive lingerie and pointed to a flat brown bag at the bottom. Judy reached for it, then peeked slowly inside as if it were booby-trapped. She eased out a red satin nightgown.

"What the hell is *that* doing in there?" I said.

Judy knelt on the floor with astonishment. "Well, Mom did say a friend stopped by a couple times a week." She laughed lightly. "No, that's not possible."

I shook my head. "Well, all I know is, she's been weird since Christmas."

Judy quickly slipped the nightgown back into the bag. "Let's make sure this stays between the two of us."

She crossed the room to a tall, narrow chest that I hoped wouldn't hold any surprises. A velvet-lined drawer contained costume jewelry Mom hadn't worn in years: circle pins, silver chains, a faux-pearl necklace. I lifted the lid of a jeweler's box and saw the diamond studs I'd given her when I could finally afford to. I recalled her swabbing their backs with alcohol and inserting them into her earlobes. "You shouldn't have," she'd cooed, but no one else, including Dad, would have indulged her.

In the drawers below, along with gloves, chiffon scarves, reading glasses, and worn leather wallets, was something I'd never seen: a thumbprint-sized pin with the initials "USN." I pictured it fastened to Dad's wool navy uniform and felt an instant chill. It wasn't until after my move to California that I learned he'd been stationed on Treasure Island in the middle of the San Francisco Bay in 1942. Now I wanted to know if he'd toured the city, tried chop suey in Chinatown or fresh crab on the wharf. A young sailor from the Midwest must have been curious, maybe even adventurous.

"I miss him," Judy said. Although I did as well, this would have broken his heart. One heart too many.

Mom's mirrored closet was as lean as the bedroom. Three gold suitcases, descending in height, stood side by side, as if waiting to be packed. Leather purses veiled with dust occupied a corner of the shelf while their matching counterparts, navy and black pumps, were on the floor. Faded khakis and T-shirts, along with Dad's brown fleece robe that Mom couldn't bear to part with, remained on the rod. I'd seen enough. "I'll be right back," I said.

I walked into the bathroom and shut the door. I was grateful for the familiar smell, a mixture of scented Kleenex and cinnamon candle. A partial tube of Colgate was on the vanity and fancy, not-to-be-used towels hung above a wicker hamper. I washed my hands, grabbed a towel, and rubbed it purposefully over my skin. *See?* I thought. *It's wet. Why aren't you here to check up on me?*

Mom's ridiculous rules swirled in my head. "No showering upstairs," she'd say each time I visited. After twenty-five years, she was still convinced steam would peel the wallpaper and moisture from the toilet would drip onto her shag carpeting. Carpet had seemed like an impractical choice for a bathroom in the first place. "I don't want to shower in the basement," I'd argue, having experienced the unpleasantness of shivering in the unheated space below us. "Your wallpaper will be completely safe if I crack the window." Once alone, however, I decided she'd never be the wiser. I undressed and quietly slid the decorator curtain across the rod.

Now, as I sat on the vanity stool, I recalled checking the floor after those showers, just in case. I knew Mom would inspect it, too.

7

Judy and I had two days to put Mom's affairs in order before our drive back to Illinois and my return trip on Amtrak. We canceled her cable, arranged a credit for the newspaper, and paid off the lawn service. Her desk calendar revealed upcoming doctor and dentist appointments, and we canceled those as well. I flipped through the previous pages, expecting to find a notation for her Easter trip to my house. There was nothing. "As if she hadn't planned on going," I said sadly to Judy.

Watching Mom's life unravel with such overwhelming speed struck me hard. I would have given anything to stop it.

"When did you go stinky last?" Mom asked while taking the sheets off my bed.

Lying was never easy. Four full days had passed. "I don't know," I said with my head down. My braids hung like ropes against my chest.

She gathered the sheets in her arms and rushed by me. "Wait in the bathroom, Connie."

My knees locked. I told myself to run and hide, but my legs weren't real legs anymore, only clumps of Play-Doh beneath my pink-checked pajamas. I remembered my accident at school, when I hadn't made it to the toilet on time. I pulled up my soiled undies, crept back to the classroom, and told Mrs. Prange I was sick. She volunteered to drive me to Grandma's house, since Mom was working. I scrunched down in her front seat, as close to the window as possible. Light-headed with shame, I prayed the smell would stay on my side of the station wagon.

Grandma C, who didn't watch us kids for any reason whatsoever, concentrated on *As the World Turns* while I lay motionless on her lumpy chestnut sofa beneath a knitted afghan. She didn't seem to notice the smell. When Mom arrived later, she understood immediately. "How could Lucille let you lie in that?" As she hurried me to the car, I regretted not having flushed my undies down Grandma's toilet.

Now I sat in the bathroom and cried. Although I'd fought off kidney disease, my body was still different from everyone else's. I wanted to be normal, to wipe with Charmin and be done with it. But no matter how hard I tried, I couldn't go.

Mom returned, carrying several feet of thin red rubber tubing. She attached one end to the faucet on the sink and stuck the other up my bottom. Cold water filled my belly, as it had many times before. I closed my eyes, and tears dripped off my chin. I imagined my insides draining away until I was empty and clean.

"Good girl," Mom said, stroking her cool hands on my hot legs. For a moment I thought she was an angel of mercy. Better late than never.

Mom's burgundy Bonneville was parked in the garage alongside a cord of firewood. "Not a scratch on it," I said, casing its perimeter. "Can you believe she was considering trading it in?"

"*What?*" Judy stuttered, the rosacea on her cheeks reappearing.

"She went to the dealer last month. Maybe she was tired of the color."

"Did they really try to sell her one?"

"I'm not sure. Mom only mentioned the new models."

Judy stormed into the kitchen. "Well, I'll find out." She threw the Yellow Pages on the counter and reached for the wall phone. Within seconds she was connected. "Did it ever occur to you that you might be taking advantage of an older woman on a fixed income?" she asked angrily. I pictured the accused in a smoke-filled office, attempting to defend himself. Judy's take-charge attitude was gratifying; Mom would be in fine hands.

When the sun woke me on our final morning, however, I felt guilty at the thought of abandoning them. Mom would remain in the hospital until Judy found an assisted-living center. All I could offer was support via telephone and frequent visits. Even though each woman had a legitimate claim to my life, my place was at home with Cara. Her birthday was the day after I returned, and everything was planned: driver's test and celebration lunch at Sweet Tomatoes, followed by a movie.

I folded my blanket, plumped the cushions on the couch, and showered. Judy and I worked steadily until noon. We emptied the refrigerator. We closed and locked windows and double-checked the sump pump in the basement. After taking one last look around, I decided the house was as immaculate as we'd found it.

"We'll be back," I said reassuringly to Judy as she placed her suitcase by the door. Her lips quivered, and I knew she was thinking ahead to the sale of the house. I wrapped my arms around her shoulders. Behind the curve of her short hair was a painting of three barn owls perched against an apricot sky. I could almost feel Mom's scathing disapproval in their round black eyes. She'd been obsessed with the possibility of failure, especially by someone other than her. Nothing we did now would please her. Yet I wanted her back, all of her, every glare and scowl, each hard-earned word of praise.

"Judy, why don't you drive Grandma and Florian home?" Mom suggested one Christmas Eve after their poker game ended.

"Sure," Judy answered, slipping her arms into a gray wool coat I loved. Since she was a sophomore in college and had several others, she sometimes lent it to me. The opportunity to imitate the sleek, fashion-model look she'd acquired with its fur-trimmed collar and sleeves was exhilarating.

"I'll go with you guys," Bill offered. Dad chuckled and said, "Me too."

We all understood Mom's motive: Dad had had a few whiskey sours. Judy was deemed most capable of driving across town and back.

Their good manners made Mom appear slightly giddy. After they left, we cleared glasses and dessert plates from the table and washed them. Then she undressed and lay in bed while I lounged on top of mine with the latest issue of *Seventeen*. The day had been satisfying, and I was reluctant to see it end. I eventually faded and switched off the lamp. My last thought was what could be keeping Judy, Bill, and Dad.

I woke abruptly to a commotion like no other, as if raving lunatics had broken in and prepared to murder us in our sleep. I was startled to realize my parents and siblings were in the middle of a fierce battle.

"All of you?" Mom bellowed. "Are you proud of yourselves coming home like common drunkards?"

"Oh, Virginia, we only had a couple," Dad swooned.

"We? *We?*" she repeated belligerently. "What's wrong with that family of yours? And Judy," she said with loathing. "Tipsy like Aunt Dorothy. Do you want to end up like her?"

I pictured them under the bright kitchen fluorescent: Dad and Judy grinning sheepishly, Bill relieved to be overlooked, though no doubt Mom was casting an evil eye in his direction as well. Their feeble attempts to explain were as effective as shoveling snow in a blizzard. Bedroom doors slammed. Mine opened, and Judy sashayed into the room, tossing her gray coat onto her bed. I said nothing. I was angry at all of them for ruining another Christmas.

Judy slowed just before the sharp curve on Highway P and turned onto the gravel path in St. John's Cemetery. I lifted the Fire and Ice roses we'd bought and examined their crimson petals, the silver striations in their core.

"Dad's getting them early," I said. We usually adorned his grave in October, the month of his passing. "Too bad Mom's not here."

Judy braked and stared out her side window. I set the foil-wrapped flowers on my lap, leaned forward, and looked beyond her. "What are those buildings?"

"You couldn't see them before," she said glumly. "The trees are gone."

I scanned the property line of the cemetery from one end to the other. The natural boundary of maples and elms had been bulldozed; piles of debris still smoldered. Nothing could have been uglier than the tall wire fence that had replaced it.

"How could they?" I said, snapping the door handle and stepping onto the pulpy spring grass. Judy snagged my arm as we walked toward our family plot, taking comfort in the Polish names of our childhood.

Suddenly, she stopped. "Not ours, too," she moaned. All that remained of the lovely old oak was a wide circle of nut-brown earth. Beside it the rust-colored granite of our grandparents' headstones and the bronze military plaques of their sons shimmered in the morning light.

I gazed up at the unobstructed cerulean sky, then divided the roses between us. Judy placed three on Florian's grave. I put the rest on Dad's. "I'm sorry," I whispered. "We're doing our best."

I had a couple miles to pull myself together before I saw Mom at the hospital, and I wasn't sure I could do it. At the corner of 9th and Racine Streets, I remembered the A&W drive-in, torn down years earlier for the Savings and Loan. In summer I'd roller-skate up to the counter and buy a stubby mug of root beer for fifteen cents. I'd order a mini-bag of popcorn for Mom, then wave good-bye to Bill, carhopping in a neat white shirt and triangular orange hat. By the time his shift ended, I was ready for bed. Mom kissed me good night with lips tasting like butter.

When we finally arrived at Theda Clark, Mom was lying on a rumpled bed by a window overlooking the Fox River and Riverside Park. Her eyes popped open as if I'd pressed a magic button.

"So, do you plan on leaving me here to rot?"

"For now you're safe, Mom. Remember? You couldn't stay in your house?" I plodded on. "We have to go today . . . "

"Me too! I can't live here forever!" Her look of annoyance changed instantly to fear.

"It won't be long," Judy said. "I'll find you a place by me."

"Why? You don't need to manage my sorry, messed-up life." Mom dropped her arms onto the blanket like withered roots left to dry. "You know, I have money. I could go anywhere. Rent an apartment, even, with less to worry about."

I was amazed by how quickly Mom slipped into and out of lucidity. "No, we've decided you can't do that," I countered.

"Oh, really!" she hissed, her anger reappearing. "*You've* decided. I don't get a say? What would your dad think of his two faultless girls now?"

"You've had a say all along," I said. "Calling 911 every time you were anxious, or couldn't breathe, or smelled gas in the house. The doctors don't want you living by yourself, and neither do we."

I glanced helplessly at Judy. She handed Mom a bag from Shopko. "New duds. Quite fashionable, don't you think?"

"Blue jeans with *elastic?*"

"Just try them on," Judy coaxed, reaching to uncover Mom's legs.

"I'm not wearing that crud!"

"Well, it's either this crud or your old crud. So this could be your brave attempt to be in style. Besides, you can't meet new people with holes in your pants."

"I don't care!" She grabbed the jeans from Judy and shot them to the floor.

Judy bent over. "Okay, fine. They'll be in the closet for when you finally get out of bed."

Mom shuddered. "Connie, don't leave me here. Please take me with you. I can't stand the thought of living in this place."

My chest hurt as I kissed her flushed cheek. "Cara's birthday is next weekend. I'll wish her a happy one from you. She'll be pleased you remembered."

Mom cried softly. In her lucid moments, she realized she wasn't going anywhere. When confused and agitated, she couldn't understand why. I wanted more than anything to turn back the years to when she was a young mother and I was her child, lying across her lap and stroking her satiny hands.

8

Judy and I hoped to finish the inventory before the auctioneer arrived at three. Although he hadn't asked for an accounting of Mom's things, it felt more reassuring to have it than not. We wouldn't be here when everything was moved to his downtown site.

Only the family and storage rooms in the basement remained. As we trudged down the wood-paneled stairway, I wondered how many times I'd done so in the past two decades. "Could you bring up some pop, Connie?" Mom used to ask when we'd sunbathe on the driveway. "I'm so thirsty I can't even spit." I'd gratefully descend into the coolness and retrieve two cans of Coke from the under-the-counter refrigerator.

Now it stood empty. The pretzel jar on the round card table did as well. The sink was dry and spotless, and the smoky glasses in the cupboard were lined up in precise dusty rows.

Judy pointed to Mom's pewter on the shelves above the wet bar. "I have those same plates."

"We all do," I said. Ever since Mom had declared her love for the precious alloy, she had insisted her children love it, too. Christmases brought bubble-wrapped candlesticks, beer steins, platters, and soup tureens. Although the fixer-upper Gary and I bought after moving to California lacked closet doors for six months, my pewter collection seemed opulent. And when a hurricane forced Bill to evacuate his rented cottage on Indian Rocks Beach, Mom was adamant. "If he has any sense at all, he'll pack his pewter."

My mother encouraged us to have "nice things." When she visited, I took her shopping at her favorite stores and boutiques. She would spot an item she liked and anticipate its place in my home. For the most part, I was practical. Objects had to be functional besides decorative. The exceptions, however, were paperweights. Whether simple crystal compositions or elaborate millefiori designs, I wholeheartedly accepted them as gifts.

The storage area was as bare as the rest of the house. Mom's seven-foot artificial Christmas tree stood in the far corner, covered with plastic. I'd seen it last in front of the picture window three years after Dad died. Her holiday spirit had reappeared in the form of red satin bows and clear lights. She'd placed shiny packages for each of us beneath its branches. Inside were Gap sweatshirts with $50 bills peeking out from under their necklines. "I didn't know what to buy," Mom had said sadly, though I'd reassured her the choice was fantastic. I appreciated another warm, fleecy layer, since we were unaccustomed to the Midwest December chill. Yet I wondered if she veered away from getting us more personal presents because she felt out of touch with our interests and our lives.

The shelves on the wall across the room were nearly empty. Where decorator boxes of Kleenex had once stood four high, there was a single roll of paper towels. I wondered how Dad would have fared if Mom had been the first to go. She often claimed he wasn't capable of taking care of himself. I didn't believe that for a second. I was certain Mom received a considerable amount of satisfaction from controlling my father.

Dad and Florian scurried down the basement steps with sloshing pails of water.

"What did you catch?" Mom asked.

"Perch, mostly," Dad hollered.

As Mom began spreading newspaper on the linoleum in front of the stove in preparation for pan-frying, I followed them. They would be in good moods after a day of fishing on the Fox River.

Dad set his pail on the laundry-room floor and pointed to my uncle. "He's a fishing genius."

"Ed, take some credit, though I admit I had the upper hand." Florian winked at me, and I smiled at being included. They shoved a pine table from its usual dark corner to the middle of the room and covered it with newspapers. Florian raised a knife, chopped off one-eyed heads, and slid the bodies over to Dad.

"Are they still alive?" I asked squeamishly from behind his denim legs.

"Barely," Florian said quickly, as if afraid to break his rhythm. *Chop, slide. Chop, slide.*

"They don't feel a thing," Dad assured me. "Same as when I snapped off those duck heads. Over and done with."

It wasn't true. My earliest childhood memory was vivid: Dad climbing the basement stairs, leaving me alone with the headless ducks. I screamed when they rose and flapped drunkenly in my direction. My three-year-old legs backpedaled, and I landed butt-first in a tub of icy water. Red, stringy necks surrounded me.

Now Dad expertly scaled the perch with a potato peeler and sliced their bloated bellies. Oozing guts made my knees weak. He placed the fish in a pail of clean water, and I carried it to the kitchen. Surely, watching Mom flour the pink slabs and arrange them in a hot, buttered skillet was preferable to butchery in the basement.

The Naperville train station was quiet for a Friday. Judy and I wheeled my two medium bags to a wood bench facing the track. We sat down and crossed our legs. We both wore loose jeans and running shoes. Neither of us spoke. I stared at the concrete, scarred by cigarette ash and winter salt, and agonized over my parting words. What could I possibly say that hadn't already been said?

The guilt of leaving was overwhelming; Mom would be alone and terrified, and Judy could do only so much. Yet I also felt a sense of relief. I'd return to the rationality of my own life. Daily routines, along with a husband and kids who were happy to see me, would provide some assurance of normalcy.

I double-checked my ticket. I retied my shoelaces. Finally, after clearing my throat a few times, I said, "I'm sure your doctor will be an excellent resource. And it's great that Marion offered to help."

Judy blew out a long breath, as if she'd been holding it forever. "Since high school, Mom's called me a flake. As if I don't have one useful brain cell. I think I'm capable of finding her a decent place to live."

"I know you are."

She blinked back tears and smiled. "Promise you'll come back."

I reached for her hand as the train from Chicago pulled in with a hot gust of wind. Letting go was as painful as peeling gauze from a day-old gash.

I shoved my suitcases into the baggage bin and collapsed into an aisle seat. The ride through Illinois was tedious: Conversing with fellow travelers seemed like a bother, and I couldn't focus on the Anne Tyler novel I'd packed. I thought about what Judy had said. Mom never gave her much credit. She was often downright harsh. I remembered one night when Judy bundled up for skating on the recently hosed ice rink at 7th Street Park. "Don't wear your new outfit and take the chance of wrecking it," Mom warned. Not only did Judy leave on the lavender ski pants and matching angora sweater, but she returned home an hour after curfew.

At breakfast the next morning, she sheepishly made her way to the table. "I have something to say," she stammered.

"I don't want to hear it," Mom steamed. "You were late again, so don't make any plans for the weekend." Then, glaring at Judy, she asked, "Did something happen to your clothes? Let me see them, *now.*"

As Judy bolted from the room, I caught a glimpse of her bandaged left hand.

"Learn from this," Mom said to Bill and me. "Do as you're told and come home where you belong, or else face the music." I nodded without hesitation.

When Judy bravely returned a minute later, the bandage was gone, exposing a jagged slash across two fingers. "Here's why I was late! Someone skated over them. I iced for the longest time, but the bleeding won't stop and they throb something awful." Her face looked like a persimmon ready to burst.

Mom appeared more sorry than I'd ever seen her. "You need stitches. Quick get dressed, and I'll drive you to the clinic."

Only a few days passed before Mom's usual self resurfaced. "Of course, you're still in trouble for breaking curfew," she reminded Judy. "Then there was all the blood I had to clean up . . . By the way, you didn't get any on your clothes, did you?"

Illinois turned into Iowa, then Nebraska, until one mile was indistinguishable from the next. A spattering of farmhouse lights, like shooting stars against a charcoal canvas, broke the monotony. While I ate chicken and dumplings in the dining car, I pictured Mom refusing her dinner tray, since her new plan of action included starving herself. I wished I could have told her to snap out of it, but I knew it wasn't that easy.

Early on, I decided never to end up like my mother. It wasn't my nature to be miserable, find fault, or cause trouble. Because I craved approval, I tried to be a perfect child. I obeyed and rarely talked back. Being the "good one" was exhausting.

Although adulthood and raising a family eased my demand for perfection, I couldn't escape it completely. I became prone to depression. Over the course of a spring and summer eight years before we moved Mom, I had a severe episode. I couldn't cope with anything—children, work, marriage. I'd grown tired of owning a business with my husband, and oftentimes our problems followed us home. Sleep was impossible, as was eating. I lost fifteen pounds. I plummeted into a jet-black hole without oxygen to fill my lungs.

One evening I confessed to Gary that I needed help and a ride to the hospital. He found a neighbor to watch the kids while I haphazardly threw clothes and their photos in a duffel. I was a mess. I couldn't even say good-bye to Ryan and Cara.

A thin-lipped woman in peach polyester admitted me. Her mouth softened like half-baked dough when I cried. She led me to a room with a bed, nightstand, and closet. The mirror on the wall was unbreakable and foggy, like the ones in gas station restrooms. A window looked out into the hallway. Passersby would discover I wasn't much to look at—just a motionless lump with swollen eyes and lips chapped as tree bark.

The following morning, there was a meeting for all the patients on the floor. "Husband's dead, sons are busy," Winnie whispered, her copper-red hair spiked every which way like the ends of a bottlebrush tree. "There's nothing to live for."

I was drawn to her soft face, grandmotherly and open. "But you're here," I said. She nodded. I thought I could learn from her: how to accept imperfection, how to be unafraid.

After the meeting, we went to the dining area, where construction paper, colored pencils, and chalk had been arranged on a folding table. "Draw or write whatever you want," a young therapist said, tucking her overgrown bangs behind her ears. "Consider poetry as a tool for opening your mind."

I remembered then how I used to love words—their form, shape, soothing sounds on my tongue. I carefully gripped a pencil; the lines came slowly, but they were there, indented and straight from one edge of the blank paper to the other. I highlighted my capital *I*'s with pink chalk. Blues swirled under my thoughts like gentle waves.

Later, I joined a group walk to a park across the street. As the sun warmed my skin on a path protected by oleanders and scrub jays, I felt hopeful of something, even if it was only my shoe touching earth. It was enough.

When we returned, I gathered my strength to wish Dad a happy birthday on the pay phone. A loudspeaker blared through the hallway, and I clasped my hand tightly over the receiver. I couldn't spoil his day. After all, I was the steady child, the one with a head on her shoulders, who had married, reared children, done all the right things. And wouldn't Mom think Grandma's illness had skipped a generation, that she'd been spared? "I don't lie in bed all day, wallowing in grief, like my mother," she used to claim. No, Mom just made sure everyone was as miserable as she was.

It felt good to stretch my legs at our first stop in Denver. Unlike at the desolate station in Naperville, people were everywhere: sidled up to a lunch counter, pressed together on church-like benches, and mobbed around a row of telephones. I dug out a calling card from my wallet and squeezed into line.

I gauged my time by the black Roman numerals on an ancient clock near the exit. Thirty minutes until departure. I'd call home, buy a magazine and a Coke with ice, then hurry back. Luckily, the conversations of the people in front of me were short.

No one answered, and I remembered it was Friday. Cara would be skating in San Jose, and Gary was at the office. I left a message: Halfway there. Tired, but the food is hot and the coach car isn't as drafty as the last trip. After I said good-bye, I was relieved they hadn't been home. They would have asked questions about Mom, and I didn't think I could summarize all I'd witnessed and felt—her sense of abandonment, my inadequacies as a daughter.

I resettled into my seat, but the train didn't budge. Passengers complained about the delay and the increasingly stale air, and I wondered why they hadn't flown instead. Yet there was no getting past the time constraint; I worried I'd miss Cara's birthday altogether.

Five hours later, a new engine and fresh crew arrived and we finally left Denver. I watched the receding skyline as we climbed the Rockies. Miniature silver boxes resembled a toddler's set of blocks waiting to be picked up, rearranged, and set down again. I remembered how I'd created my own world when I was young, raking maple leaves into the walls of a mansion. A small mound became a fireplace, a thick layer my featherbed. I hosted garden parties among the dazzling reds and yellows and twirled beneath the afternoon sky. I finally had something all to myself, at least until the wind rose or my brother appeared, eager for annihilation.

Seasons rewound outside the car's fingerprinted windows. Tender buds were replaced by barren trees, then rocks and a dusting of snow. I couldn't clear my head of Mom. I saw her reaching across the hospital bed and jabbing Judy in the arm. "How did your hair get so gray if you don't have anything to worry about? Look at mine—white, from so many problems. I'll bet Dad was glad to trade it all in. I should be so lucky."

In Naperville, Judy had breezily referred to Mom as "our little lunatic," and I'd laughed. Now I felt sickened by complicity. Besides pain, we were all she had.

Mom and Dad never seemed to have much time for socializing. They watched TV after washing the supper dishes. On weekends they busied themselves with household chores. Some Saturdays Dad golfed eighteen holes with his work buddies. He was a terrific golfer, even with a metal plate in one wrist from a bout of TB.

Once a month, they played poker with two other couples. When the game was in our kitchen, I'd lie in bed and listen to their easygoing commentary about each other's playing ability, or lack thereof. Golf-club swizzle sticks clinked against highball glasses, and fresh coffee popped in the percolator. As the smell of warm ham slipped under my door, I felt safe within the yellow walls of my room.

Poker and occasional family gatherings with Grandma C, Florian, and Rosemary were the extent of Mom's socializing. She didn't speak of girlfriends or shop with anyone but us. I concluded she wasn't fond of other women. One neighbor, who also had three children, seemed like an ideal candidate to gossip with. But Mom avoided her, claiming the husband was a drunk and the daughter a boy-chaser, a regular Queen of Sheba.

Another neighbor, a tall, slender woman with a slight masculine swagger, drove Mom crazy. "Dennis, bring me my clippers!" she'd yell from under a wide-brimmed straw hat shading her bare shoulders. Mom would slam the living-room window shut and say, "I'm not listening to that screeching. And wearing a colored bra, for God's sake."

Dad would chuckle, "Oh, Virginia, it's just a bathing suit." I admired the woman's confident stride and enormous smile. She had the whitest teeth I'd ever seen.

All the neighborhood ladies bothered Mom. My best friend's mother was too quiet, another had a horsey laugh, and the poor wife in the corner house was her husband's slave. I wasn't sure how a woman was supposed to act.

Ultimately, I settled on a cross between the housewives on television and in the movies, and those I observed in real life. I emulated

Maureen O'Hara in *Miracle on 34th Street,* who learned to be generous, positive, and open-minded. I vowed never to be submissive or, worse yet, overbearing.

The Salt Lake City station was the approximate size of a small-town diner. Its two vending machines offered coffee and snacks. I feasted on peanut M&M's before dialing Judy's number.

"Assisted living is so expensive, Con." I could hear her shuffling papers. "One place wants five thousand a month, thirty-two hundred if we agree to a roommate and less care."

I did the math in my head: Mom's money would run out in a few short years. Even with an Alzheimer's diagnosis, I expected she'd live well into her nineties like her paternal aunts. However, they were Notre Dame nuns and I was certain Mom wouldn't age as gracefully. She used to say, "Getting old is degrading. You lose your looks, then body parts fail. You might even go crazy, like Grandma. The best thing is if life just ends."

By the time I said good-bye to Judy, I was practically ready to give up myself. Then I decided to make one more call.

Mom picked up more quickly than I'd expected. "Connie? Where are you? I'm having the worst day. Please get me out of here!"

"Not until you eat," I said sternly. "Not until you're stronger." My newest heartache, the realization that our mother-daughter roles had completely reversed, took less than a minute.

9

Miles from our scheduled refueling in Sparks, Nevada, the train abruptly stopped. Everyone groaned. "Now what?" barked a woman I'd seen chain-smoking in the club car. From the back a gruff voice yelled, "Look out the window, for Pete's sake!" On a deserted strip of road, an ambulance with flashing red lights sped toward us. When it parked by the dining car, I wondered if someone had choked on their lunch. Paramedics lugged gear up the steps, then descended minutes later with an elderly man strapped to a gurney. I fell into my seat and one of my blackest memories.

We'd been shoe shopping at Mervyns on the warm June morning of my thirty-fourth birthday. "Your dad doesn't feel well," Mom sighed. "He wants to go home."

I observed him above boxes of Reeboks and was startled by the color of his cheeks, like Earl Grey tea that's sat way too long. I briefly considered calling 911, but that meant finding a phone, or a clerk, and I didn't think there was time. Then I remembered the urgent-care facility across the street. I grabbed two-year-old Cara and rushed over to him.

Dad looked at me weakly, and I talked fast. "Go with Mom. I'll get the van." Cara struggled when I tucked her against my ribs like a football and ran through the parking lot. She defiantly kicked off her purple jellies as I buckled her in. When I turned and saw my parents shuffling toward the curb, I forced down the bile that had risen in my throat.

Dad was damp and heavy, but we managed to lift him onto the high bucket seat. "You okay?" I asked. He winced. My hands clamped the steering wheel as the van lurched forward. I was terrified I'd made the wrong decision.

As we stumbled through the clinic's entrance, a woman with a mousy bun pinned to the top of her head sprang up from behind the front desk. She waved us to a room, and within seconds a doctor appeared, placing a round tablet under Dad's tongue. "Nitroglycerin," he said calmly. Mom was dazed, and I nudged her into a chair. Cara tearfully circled my knees. I gave Dad an encouraging smile, then carried her to the waiting room. While she stacked Legos, I silently counted the strokes in his family: Grandpa, Dorothy, Florian. I stared at the clock, its minute hand adhered to the flat face like tar.

The woman and Mom returned, their arms oddly linked. I'd never seen my mother so meek as when she requested some water. "Your daughter should say good-bye first." She opened a back door. Through the glare of noontime sun, I spotted Dad, lying in an ambulance with the doctor by his side. I raised my hand; I wasn't sure he saw me.

We dropped Cara at a neighbor's and drove to the hospital where they'd taken Dad. "He's prepped for surgery," the receptionist said. "Can you fill out his paperwork?" Mom didn't answer. I volunteered, insisting she go to Dad. "Hurry!" I said as she balked.

After finishing, I found them: Dad wired to an IV and heavily sedated, Mom glued to the floor a foot away. Nothing, however, could have prepared me for the scathing remarks of the surgical nurse. "99.9 percent blocked. Looks like you'll quit those cigarettes now, huh, Ed?"

His tired eyes caught mine. I patted his cold arm, reassuring him we'd be here. But after he was wheeled away, Mom said, "Let's go home, Connie. I'm exhausted." My face burned as if I'd been slapped. Leave while Dad's chest was split in half? I felt regrettably traitorous as we walked to the van. I still couldn't say no to my mother.

We learned the results the next morning: a successful quadruple bypass with thirteen separate connections. Dad looked like someone else's father as he slept, swollen, skin taut and mottled as a tree frog's. I touched his wrist. Blood pumped in his overworked veins, and I realized how much I loved him. Unconditionally. The same love I had for the woman now leaning against me.

"Isn't it great that Bill's here?" I asked Mom. The weight on my shoulders had lifted the moment he'd exited the baggage claim at the airport.

She nodded with her eyes closed. It was eerie to see my brother in Dad's spot at my kitchen table. At thirty-eight he resembled him more than ever: square-jawed, straight-shouldered, and sturdy. Mom blotted her teary face with a tissue. "You two talk back and forth like I don't exist."

"We need to decide where Dad's going to recuperate," Bill answered in a serious tone. "We're waiting for you to voice an opinion."

"Whatever you want, I don't care," she said.

"We could avoid a nursing home if he stays here," Bill continued matter-of-factly. "He'd be comfortable in a hospital bed. You'd have to drive him to checkups, Connie, set up physical therapy. It won't be easy, but it would be ideal."

Mom covered her face with her hands. I knew the decision was mine. "We'll make it work," I offered. Six weeks in my house could mean a quicker recovery and even quality bonding with the kids. I tried not to visualize all the problem scenarios. However, Mom's silver hair, frizzy from the heat, was a reminder of how unhappy she'd be without air-conditioning.

We picked Dad up from the hospital on the first day of Ryan's summer vacation. It almost felt as if nothing had happened, that we were simply on another shopping trip. I drove slowly and carefully, glancing often at Dad sitting beside me. His hair was shaggy, and his pale face bore traces of gray stubble he'd missed with the razor. I recalled how he'd wanted to shave a week ago, when his unsteady fingers had looked as if they'd do more harm than good. "Take a day off," Bill had said cheerfully. Now I noticed the deep red ridge on Dad's chest, extending from his stiff collar to the first button and beyond. I was aware of every groove in the pavement and sway of the van.

At home we entrenched ourselves in new routines. Each morning Mom made Dad's breakfast while I drove the kids to swimming lessons.

Upon returning, she'd itemize the details of those trying hours. After lunch, she rested and I took over. "Cara, hand Grandpa his breathing tube and watch him raise the little ball," I'd say. She did while giggling at his hollowed cheeks. "Okay, tell Grandpa it's naptime." She'd kiss his forehead and run to her room.

But instead of sleeping, she'd dismantle her drawers and closet, scattering clothes, shoes, and toys. Although my impatience soared with the afternoon temperature, I settled for disorder. I needed the normal sounds of life, even dogs barking from one end of the block to the other, children shrieking on a Slip 'N Slide.

By the third week Dad got himself out of bed and made his way to the living room for physical therapy. He lay on the couch and wearily lifted his calves as a therapist counted repetitions. Cara stretched alongside him on the floor, flailing her stubby legs with abandon. In the evenings, the pained look on Dad's face lessened, although his eyes seemed focused on something other than the Hawaiian landscape of *Magnum, P.I.* While he lounged in my Danish chair by the patio door, Ryan refilled his water glass and Cara held his hand. I was astonished by their gentleness. Even Mom relaxed, exceeding my expectations by hardly complaining about the stagnant air and eventually dozing off.

One day after an appointment with Dad's surgeon, a neighbor skipped across her manicured lawn to my side of the van and blushed. "Your mom had a slight problem. David tried to help."

I couldn't imagine what she meant until I walked in the house. On Gary's newly tiled entry was a half inch of standing water. I heard a steady sloshing from down the hall.

"What happened?" I yelled, peering around the corner.

Mom was on her knees. Ryan and Cara stood wide-eyed in their bedroom doorways. Mounds of wet towels sank into the brown carpet.

"The toilet ran over," Mom said. "I suppose *you* would have known how to turn off the water."

I woke up in my own bed on Cara's sixteenth birthday. I was relieved to be home, to kiss Gary good morning, to hear our parakeet chirping and the clothes dryer thumping. Even the drone of a lawn mower was oddly comforting. Yet I didn't think I could celebrate wholeheartedly. All I had to give Cara was myself, overtired and drained. But when she hugged me and didn't let go, I knew she was satisfied.

Judy called the next day with the results of her assisted-living search. She was most impressed with Brighton Gardens, a brand-new facility one mile from her house. "Three stories overlooking a golf course. A large foyer on the first floor opens into a living area done in blues, mauves, and yellows. The dining room has round tables with white linen napkins and tablecloths. Residents order from a menu just as if they were in a restaurant. It's all about maintaining their dignity." She took a breath.

"Sounds great so far," I said.

"It gets better. A beauty parlor on-site and movies every night at six. Tomorrow I'll fax you a floor plan. I think *I* could live there, Con."

"You and me both," I laughed. "We could be roommates again."

After we hung up, I thought about how Mom's life had changed. She wanted to keep relatively little: her teddy bears, her rocker, the ivory afghan Rita had crocheted, a delicate needlepoint, one wreath, and several framed photographs. She'd part with almost everything else, except her favorite brass pieces, which she'd asked Judy to store in her garage. I couldn't picture Mom living in one room, or possibly sharing it with another lady. Her personality would need a complete overhaul mighty quick.

I never understood why Mom didn't like other women. She'd grown up in a female household: three sisters, mother, grandmother. In photos they seemed happy: Mom and Grandma on a porch swing with their buff-colored Pekingese. Sisters in identical floor-length gowns, velvet bows at their waists and guitars on their laps. Yet I imagined the sibling rivalries: who stayed home to watch the youngest, who climbed the stairs with Grandma's dinner tray, who scraped the crusty dishes.

When I was young, Mom even found fault with my best friend's mother, the nicest person on our block and Dad's cousin besides. "Why do you always play there?" she'd ask after I returned from playing Barbie all morning. I wanted to say because friends weren't allowed in our house, but I didn't. I couldn't admit how comfortable and safe they made me feel.

I believed her family was better than ours. Standing at their back door, looking through the screen into the kitchen, I saw the supper table set for five and heard quiet conversation from the TV room. Soon they'd talk over roast beef and enjoy homemade chocolate cake. They'd say please and thank you, all the politeness missing from our gloomy meals. Although I didn't know if Pam's parents ever argued in front of her and her brothers, I was certain they hadn't maintained a code of strict silence for two weeks straight. I longed to open their door and invite myself in, reside in the teeny back room. Being a first cousin once removed, I thought I might qualify.

"She's in," Judy said a few days later when I picked up my extension at work. "So I bought a twin bed, dresser, and nightstand. Dark wood with brass accents. The store delivers. I'll drive to Mom's Friday night, pack the rest of her stuff, and return with her on Saturday. And the best part is, Marion's coming along."

"Ah," I laughed, "a buffer." Judy and I had concluded long ago that an extra person in the mix, especially someone naturally gregarious like Judy's friend Marion, made difficult situations with Mom more bearable. I'd often relied on my mother-in-law to fill that position; Bev was quite capable of standing up to Mom, or at the very least softening her blows.

The week before my junior prom, Mom, Judy, and I went to a for-mal-wear shop. "We're looking for a white gown," Mom announced cheerfully to an immaculately coiffed salesclerk.

"Lovely," she chirped, raising her perfectly arched brows. She pressed a tape measure around my flat chest, and I disliked her imme-diately. When she disappeared among the rows of frilly dresses, I said, "Why does it have to be white? I'm so thin I'll look like a slice of Wonder bread!"

"Because you need to be different from the other girls," Mom answered firmly. "After all, you are the *prom queen*."

Her emphasis on those words, at a volume for everyone outside the dressing room to hear, made me cringe. I hoped for support from

Judy, but she flipped through a *Glamour* and didn't look up. I wondered if Mom would ever stop making decisions for us.

The clerk returned with three white dresses draped over her silk-sleeved arm. I tried on two, and thankfully Mom and I agreed on their status: ill-fitting and ostentatious. The third dress, however, was another story. "Lace eyelet," Mom beamed, "and it fits so well."

I couldn't take my eyes off my skinny arms and the pea-green ribbon encircling the empire waist. "It itches," I groaned. "And it's ugly. Aren't there any others?"

The clerk, hovering just beyond the curtain, said she'd check. But Mom's mind was set. "For one thing, it's the right price. When Mrs. Scovy shortens it, she can attach a more flattering ribbon."

I could feel tears beginning to form. I'd been embarrassed before, wearing Judy's hand-me-down to the homecoming dance; it was a giant doily, yellow as Grandma's canary. This time I dreamed of a light blue satin gown with tiny pearls dotting the bodice and cap sleeves.

"Connie, stop pouting. You're too old for that." She stuck her head outside the curtain. "Excuse me. We've decided on this one."

I pulled on my clothes and stormed out of the store. I leaned on a parking meter and sobbed. How was I going to stand before my classmates in that horrendous dress?

When I finally got home, Gary picked me up in his '56 Chevy and we drove to his house. I sank into a chair and cried in front of him and his mother.

"I'll admit I wouldn't force my children to wear something they hated," Bev said, clearly irritated. Then, in a soothing voice, she added, "Perhaps you can fix it so you'll at least be comfortable."

I wanted to stay in her living room forever.

"I'm taking Mom for a perm before we leave Saturday," Judy continued. "She refuses to get one at Brighton Gardens."

"That will have to change *really* fast," I said.

"But what I need to talk to you about, Con . . . " She hesitated, then blurted, "I have to sign resuscitation orders. Mom doesn't have a terminal illness, so if anything happens, I think we want her resuscitated."

I shoved aside the pile of bills I'd been working on. "I never thought otherwise. After all, she's simply changing residences."

"Right," Judy chuckled. "Except she'll be surrounded by little old ladies and wheelchairs and complain even more about how decrepit she is. She says, 'Why don't you let me die?' I say, 'Die of what?' You can't just invent something."

"Strong parents never die," I laughed. "They stick around to make sure we don't slip up, or maybe, in some cases, to hold us up. Did I ever tell you how Mom sent me tulips on Valentine's Day the year I was so depressed? With a note that read: 'Be thankful for all you have.' Too bad she can't follow her own advice."

10

The auctioneer wasn't the businesslike note-taker I'd expected. Dressed in khaki shorts, a loose cotton shirt, and sandals, Tom scanned Mom's house like a tourist on vacation. "Everything gets moved to a warehouse. I focus on display to emphasize the value of each item."

I nodded politely, but the idea made me nauseous.

"We'd like to keep a few pieces," Judy interrupted.

"No problem," Tom said, slightly bowing his balding head. "As long as they're removed from the house beforehand."

I unclenched my teeth. "Can you give us an estimate?"

"Furniture and paintings, of course, will bring the most. That brass platter," he said, pointing to the kitchen, "maybe fifty dollars, but don't count on it. People want bargains. I'd say somewhere around five thousand."

I regarded Judy's flushed cheeks and sensed a mutual hesitation. Financially, the estimate seemed too low. Besides her car and her house, Mom's belongings were her only source of revenue. But the more troubling issue was, how does one quantify a life? Any amount would be Lilliputian compared with the knowledge, experiences, and achievements of seventy-seven years.

But there was nothing else to do. Judy and I signed the agreement, and Tom scheduled the auction for the third Saturday in September.

We stood quietly at the screen door as Tom backed his Ford Ranger down the driveway. Judy stared at the receipt in her hand, and I instantly felt a new flash of guilt. I wasn't returning for the auction.

Judy would witness the sale of Mom's belongings without me by her side. I yearned to be an exemplary sister.

With a couple of daylight hours remaining, we dragged lawn chairs from the garage to the yard. Under a clump of birch, I remembered the last time I'd been here: Dad's seventy-third birthday, a July afternoon three months before he passed away.

Dad and I had munched popcorn and chatted periodically. His beige polo had risen and fallen slowly with each labored breath of his concave chest. I'd been amazed by how content he seemed, even though he knew he had a short time to live.

How sad and ironic, I realized now, to be sitting beneath the same trees and dealing with the decline of another parent. A postal truck turned onto the lane, spewing loose gravel into the ditch by Mom's mailbox. I could almost hear her yelling at the kids who jumped off the school bus and lobbed stones at it just for fun.

"Our last day," I sighed to Judy, "and our last supper. How about Blier's?"

Besides serving the best fish fry in the area, the restaurant had one other claim to fame: The owner's son was a professional football player in the sixties. In our part of the world, that was a particularly big deal, although he hadn't played for our beloved Green Bay Packers.

"I'm buying," Judy said, combing her fingers through her recent razor cut. "God, I'm tired. This job keeps getting harder."

I thought we'd been thorough, assembling mementos on the dining room table for everyone. Bill requested only the seascape he'd painted. We added Dad's Navy pin, a keepsake for our nephew, christened with the middle name Edward. Cara wanted a blue fleece blanket Mom used solely when we visited, and Ryan expressed interest in the blender. Judy and I chose photographs for all of us, along with an uncle's paintings and a few odds and ends. I wondered if it was enough. Yet our choices for something personal were few. In the past year Mom had donated clothing to Goodwill and disposed of what she considered "clutter." Because there was little left, every item felt like a treasure. It was heartbreaking to leave anything behind.

The following morning, I set my laptop on the redwood picnic table in the garage and waited for Judy to finish her coffee. This part of the inventory would be simple. Shovels, rakes, and brooms hung on the right wall, and a stack of firewood lined the left. After Dad had died, Mom had been reluctant to use the fieldstone fireplace. I was certain a cousin who lived nearby would gladly take the wood.

The burgundy Bonneville, dust covered without its weekly wash, sat regally in the middle. Mom and Dad bought a new car every four years at first, and then, as they got older, every two. The monstrous Impala I learned to drive on was replaced with an even more enormous Grand Prix by the time I graduated from high school. For twenty years they traded up for fresh shades of bronze, tan, and, once, a steely gray. Mom was rarely as happy as when she'd call with the news.

My brother-in-law, who owned a car dealership, agreed to buy the Bonneville. Judy and I were ecstatic. The money would cover almost six months of expenses at Brighton Gardens. I tried not to dwell on the fact that Mom's total assets would be eaten away in a few years.

In the far corner behind the garbage cans were Bill's old bat, glove, and grass-stained hardball. I was surprised Mom had saved them; perhaps she'd had her grandchildren in mind. Yet I couldn't recall the kids throwing or hitting in her heavily landscaped yard. They would have loved ours on State Street, tailor-made for baseball, unencumbered by trees, fences, or boundaries of any kind for three houses down. A home-run ball rolled clear to the end of the block without so much as a twig to stop it.

Judy broke my reverie as the screen door slammed behind her. She instantly spotted the ancient radio console in which Mom stored garden tools and clothespins. "Ah, Grandma's Bendix. Look. It even has a turntable. Remember the 78s she played?"

I didn't recollect the music Grandma C liked, but I could place the console in her parlor, sleek with polish and topped with figurines.

"Aunt Dorothy loved to jitterbug," Judy smiled. "I can still see her with a cocktail in one hand and a cigarette in the other, tapping her open-toed pumps to Tommy Dorsey."

Because I was six years younger than Judy, I saw only our aunt's lips: two wide crescents of flame. When I was a teenager, she suffered a stroke. Yet she was still able to travel from Des Moines with Uncle Hank and my cousins for Grandma's funeral. I hadn't known which was sadder: Grandma gone or Dorothy slouched in a chair half-paralyzed and nonverbal in a cotton housedress at the age of fifty-two. Her mouth hung, pinkish lipstick caked in its corners.

"Let's put the radio in your car," I suggested.

"Okay," Judy sighed. "Everything seems so final, like we're stripping the house bare."

"In another month it will be, whether we like it or not." The truth was brutal. We'd reached the end of our family as we knew it. I looked at her apologetically, then stood and pressed the garage-door button. From a few blocks away, I heard the faint rumbling of engines on Highway P, a two-lane county road that had connected Mom to her world. I recalled her hesitation before entering traffic. "All clear," I'd say after glancing both ways. She'd turn her head back and forth until the gap between cars was astronomical. Now the neighborhood was quiet. Amid the scent of fresh-cut grass and clover, it seemed almost like any other summer day.

The weekend Judy moved Mom to Illinois was excruciatingly long. Laundry and sloppy bathrooms from a week's absence kept me busy, but my mind had never left Mom's house. I wanted to stand beside her at the window and watch spring bunnies scamper among budding bushes. I wanted to deal a hand of cards and hear her criticize my ragged cuticles. I wanted to catch her napping upright on the love seat, her head bobbing in a vain attempt to protect her weekly hairdo.

Judy called Sunday night, sounding hoarse and worn out. "Mom never asked to see the house. I had plenty of reasons ready why she shouldn't."

I pictured my sister lying in her usual spot for our conversations—flat on her dining room floor. Rosie, her large cat, with the distinct black-and-white markings of a newborn calf, would tap at the stretched phone cord like a toy.

"That place does something to me, Con. I see both Mom and Dad there. When I locked the door, I lost it."

"I would have, too."

"And she was so complacent during the drive—until we crossed the state line. Then she shook like a madwoman."

All the muscles in my body seemed to tense. "What did you do?"

"Gave her an Ativan. It kicked in fast. When we arrived at Brighton Gardens, she was as gracious as could be."

"Sounds too good to be true."

"Well, it didn't last. She had a panic attack while unpacking. I told her the move was a change for the better. You should have seen her: prone on the bed, staring at the ceiling, chanting, 'I will not be afraid. I will not be afraid.'"

"I'll be damned," I said. "Mom's never been afraid of anything."

You wouldn't have known it was lunchtime by the sky beyond my bedroom window—black as Mom's cast-iron skillet. "Connie, come on!" she yelled.

I dashed into the kitchen with Little Miss Kay. Mom hovered in the doorway, windblown and out of breath. Socks and T-shirts spilled from the counter. It looked like she'd unclipped the laundry from the clothesline just in time.

"Let's go," she said, motioning me forward with a flashlight.

I followed small circles of light down the basement steps. The linoleum was cold for June, and I regretted not having slipped on my sneakers. Behind us, the screen door banged. I pictured it ripping from its hinges and somersaulting into the neighbor's yard.

My siblings huddled on scatter rugs under the Ping-Pong table. I crawled between them. "We'll be fine," Mom cried over the rain that lashed narrow panes of glass by the ceiling. I wasn't so sure—one storm had sliced our elm tree in half. I plugged my ears and prayed it would blow into the next county.

Suddenly, Mom shoved the flashlight into my trembling hand. "Aim it at the floor by the chimney," she said, taking off toward the laundry room. I did as I was told. Then I saw it—water, glistening in the broken beams and heading in our direction. "Help!" Mom ordered when she reappeared with pails and rags. Judy and Bill sprang into action. They mopped and squeezed rags as fast as they could. "Over there!" Mom bellowed when the river changed course. As they jumped into position, I dropped Little Miss Kay and couldn't move the flashlight to find her. I imagined Dad coming home from work and finding four bodies and one plastic baby doll floating under a foot of water.

Then a lightning bolt lit the room. "I think we're winning," Mom said, and they worked even harder. Judy's bangs stuck to her forehead. Bill took off his shirt and emptied one pail after another. For the first time, he looked like a man—confident, like Mom. I didn't think I'd ever be as fearless.

I tried to picture Mom lying between new sage-green sheets, but I couldn't. I saw her rigid beneath a saffron spread, listening to the grandmother clock chime each hour in the living room. "It's a sign from your dad," she'd said, claiming the previously broken clock had worked only after he'd died. Although I had my doubts, I did nothing to convince her otherwise. What harm could it do, I reasoned, if she was amused and comforted as well?

During the second week, Mom was given a roommate. When Anna moved into the other half of the two-bedroom suite, she and her children greeted Mom graciously. Mom reacted with a snooty *hmpf* and a hefty door slamming. I felt sorry for Anna and her family.

One night she wandered accidentally into Mom's room after she'd fallen asleep. Mom screamed when Anna loomed beside her bed. She buzzed the aide on duty and demanded he remove her. "Unbelievable," Judy said afterward. "Mom thought she was going to get slugged. I told her Anna was confused and still adjusting."

Yet the image evoked what I'd witnessed more than thirty years before, in our kitchen on State Street: Mom cowering under the raised fist of my teenage brother. She begged him to put down the wood ruler he'd cocked just above her shoulder. I had no idea what transpired between them. But I'd never seen such rage in Bill's eyes, and I wasn't certain he could contain it. When he finally slammed the ruler on the counter and ran out of the house, Mom sank onto the gray linoleum and sobbed. Her tears became mine, her body a grown-up, vulnerable version of my own. By suppertime, life returned to normal. The five of us sat, as usual, in silence. As far as I knew, Mom never mentioned the incident to anyone. Bill and I didn't discuss it either.

"I couldn't find her," Judy huffed as if she were still at Brighton Gardens, searching for our mother. "She wasn't in her room. I circled the entire floor until I heard someone retching in the Country Kitchen. It was Mom!"

My prolapsed mitral valve flip-flopped in my chest. "She's sick?" I blew out an expansive breath, hoping to slow it.

"She refused the fruit cocktail an aide was trying to feed her. So I took over. Picture this, Con. With each spoonful I said, 'Chew, swallow.' She glared and snarled, 'You old dog.' Well, I'd had it and answered, 'Arf arf.'"

We both laughed. "My God, Jude, the things you have to do."

"That's not all," she said. "I'm out of her will. And she wants to be hooked up to a feeding tube."

I suddenly felt quite sober. "Some imagination. Is she not eating for effect, or is something physically wrong?"

"I'll know more after she sees the doctor. For now, it's looking grim. When I told her I'd come tomorrow, she asked if she'd still be alive."

I was startled yet instantly remembered a scene from when I was in my twenties. Mom had been folding laundry when she said, "I considered taking my own life when I was younger." I was so taken aback that I couldn't respond. Without even looking up from the towels on her bed, she continued, "I decided against it because of you kids."

I'd felt violated by Mom's matter-of-fact and callous admission. She had never opened up to me before, not on any level. She'd revealed something no mother should utter to her child.

The doctor determined Mom was severely dehydrated and transferred her to the hospital.

"Pitiful," Judy said. "The single thing she cares about is the husband of the poor woman in the bed next to her. She's got mouth cancer. He showed her how to sip from a straw. Mom says to him, 'You can fix my bedsores anytime.' Can you imagine? She's too antsy to get bedsores. And what does she plan on doing with the man with his wife just a few feet away?"

I couldn't imagine my mother flirting with anyone. Yet she claimed all the men at Brighton Gardens had their eyes on her. She loved the attention so much that one of Judy's friends called Mom a living Lolita.

"She's sure gutsy," I said. "What's the doctor's plan?"

"IVs, blood work, abdominal CAT scan. If the tests are negative, he'll move her to psych. He says she playacts most of the time. I could have told him *that*. When the physical therapist asked Mom to exercise her legs, she kicked them up and down to beat the band. When he left, she pulled the blanket over her head and cried."

I thought about the movie Judy and I had irreverently cast the year before. We called it *Our Little Lunatic,* with Anne Bancroft playing Mom and Jane Fonda as Judy, since Dad had always claimed a resemblance between Judy and Jane. Judy suggested the other Fondas as well: Peter for Bill, Bridget for me. I laughed and said she'd need a ton of makeup, since I was so much older. I felt horrible at Mom's expense, but the comic relief did wonders.

A few days later, Mom declined the liquid for the CAT scan and Judy was asked to intervene. "I explained the procedure at least ten times," Judy said. "She finally started sipping and talked, and before you know it, she's telling me about parking at the Neenah Point with her first boyfriend."

"Ah, those men again," I chuckled.

"Really, I was so exhausted afterward, I sat in my car. Mom understands her brain's all mixed up and there's nothing she can do about it."

Mom picked up the phone on the sixth ring, her voice as fuzzy as our connection.

"Oh, Connie, it's you! Where are you? I don't like it here. I don't know what I'm doing."

"Just a while longer, Mom. You'll be released soon, and then you can go back to your new home."

"My home? In Wisconsin?"

"No, Mom. Brighton Gardens." I enunciated the words more slowly than I'd intended.

"Connie, I think I'm seeing things: black guys, red guys, and every color in between. A black nurse drew enough blood from my arm, you'd swear he was milking a cow!"

"They're checking to see if you're sick," I said. "Let them do their jobs."

"I am, but I can't stand these people."

Her intolerance for ethnic diversity hadn't changed and was definitely being challenged. I remembered one of her first visits to California. "Look at all those Orientals," she'd said, her mouth agape, as if in the presence of aliens. It didn't matter if a waiter at Sizzler was Mexican or Filipino; she made no distinctions—they were all "colored." I told her to keep her comments to herself, or at least not to make them within earshot of the victims or her grandchildren. She raised her eyebrows as if she had no idea what I meant.

"Promise me you'll eat, Mom," I chided now. "Whatever they bring you. It's absolutely necessary that you eat to stay alive."

"Any fool knows that," she answered.

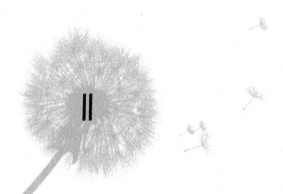

II

I could paper the walls of an average-sized house with the number of X-rays performed on my immediate family. Sometimes I already knew the obvious: my teenage son's broken leg during soccer practice, his right foot twisted and pointing downfield instead of straight up at the suppertime sky. Other incidents required more investigation. I insisted on a second X-ray when pain surged through my daughter's back after she fell while performing a double axel. Then there it was, in the glow of a rectangular light panel—a hairline fracture of the T12 vertebra.

When I got the news that Mom's X-rays showed an inflamed gallbladder, I wasn't surprised. That explained her loss of appetite and abdominal discomfort. Her gallbladder was removed, and I envisioned her entire life being turned upside down again.

I called the day after surgery. "How are you feeling, Mom?"

"Ugh," she groaned. "But my surgeon's cute and the nurses are kind. I can't ask for much more."

I thought I was talking to an impostor, since compliments and cheerfulness were rare commodities after her move. If pain medication was responsible, I wanted it included in her daily schedule. She needed a break from negativity, and so did the rest of us.

"I'm forty-eight today," I said. "Thanks for all you've done for me."

"Oh," Mom sighed. "I didn't send a card. It's sunny here, like the day you were born." She was silent for a moment, then whispered conspiratorially, "My roommate is from India. You should see all the colored faces that pass our doorway."

"That's really interesting," I said, nixing any further pronouncements of her prejudices. Yet I was amazed at her roller-coaster mind, shifting quickly from one topic to the next.

"Hmongs fill our mall now, whole gangs of them. . . . I can't even remember the last time I was there." As her voice trailed off, I remembered distinctly.

"We're meeting for lunch," I'd said to her from my room at Woodfield Suites during a visit to the Fox Valley just two years earlier. "Gary's folks, even Rita and Don. Drive to the mall around noon. We'll be in the food court. You can't miss us." I laughed while picturing our entourage—aunts, uncles, cousins, grandparents. We'd stand together and consider our dining options: Subway, McDonald's, and Panda Express, no doubt a recent addition to accommodate the growing ethnic diversity of the area. One by one we'd break off to place our orders, then carry our trays to a conclave of tables in the center of the court.

As I bit into a turkey and cheese, I spotted Mom buying a sandwich. She studied the crowd but didn't see us. She pulled out a chair at the far end of the room, as if that had been her intention all along. I rose and walked toward her. She looked like any other elderly woman, alone with her midday meal and her thoughts. Had she misunderstood me earlier, or was she impatient to eat? There didn't seem to be a logical explanation.

Now, as I listened to her ramble on about Indians and Hmongs, I realized her confusion at the mall had been another sign of dementia. I wondered how many others I'd missed.

Several days after the gallbladder operation, Judy found Mom strapped to a hospital bed. "She won't stay put," Judy said, clearly exasperated. "And she's throwing whatever she can get her hands on."

I twisted the phone cord between my fingers and pictured Mom, veins pulsing purple in her temples.

"She also accused me of being after her money! Can you believe it? Oh, and I'm a rotten person, and Dad must be glaring down at me for treating her so badly. Thank God the doctor ordered a major tranquilizer."

"Mom didn't hit anyone, did she?"

"No, nothing like that. But any chance of rationality has been shot to hell. Worse yet, she's aware of the fact that she's losing her mind."

Judy's words felt like thirty-pound weights. I repeated them slowly to myself.

"When I told her I was going home, she thought I meant Green Bay. How many years have I been in Illinois? Twenty-five? Yet she remembers how hard she was on Bill and admits her expectations of him were too high."

"Has she ever offered that to Bill? She'd call him a genius. We know he's smart, but what pressure." I'd envied how easily everything came to my brother. I'd prayed for teachers other than his so my average report cards wouldn't be compared with his superior ones. To top it off, he could sing—a talent I'd longed for. I still saw Bill with his crew cut and bow tie, standing in the middle of St. John's gym and crooning "O Tannenbaum" to a packed house of Catholic children and nuns.

"I'm sure she hasn't," Judy said, "just as she's never given me any credit for having a brain."

"Or me for doing what was best for my family. Her world stopped when we moved to California and took Ryan away. Not once did she say, 'I'm glad Gary found a good job.' Oh God, here I go—water under the bridge."

"Well, all I know," Judy sighed, "is when I look into those ghastly white eyes, I wonder, Who *is* she?"

"I doubt even Mom has ever figured that out."

I couldn't get through my daily routine without thinking of Mom. She was everywhere: reading headlines aloud at the breakfast table, watching me make tacos for supper. I'd slice a tomato, set the knife down, and gasp at the idea of Mom tied to her bed like an animal. I'd stir ground round with onions and green peppers and hear her scream in frustration. I'd stuff a warmed taco shell with lettuce, meat, and cheese and recall her turned-up nose at "Mexican" food, although my bland rendition was nothing more than her beef casserole without the egg noodles. The categories under which I filed images of her all my adult life—Angry Mom, Fatalistic Mom, Pathetic Mom—seemed exceedingly simplistic and maybe even heartless. I'd have to come up with a different system quickly, or risk being sucked down a black hole of my own.

I was collating an arithmetic workbook for second graders when my boss tapped me on the shoulder. I felt lucky on this stuffy June morning to be assigned piecemeal work instead of cutting books off sewing machines, like the other college kids. That was ridiculously fast and tedious: separating, jogging, and loading skids while women stormed thread through paper. I often wondered if anyone noticed the tiny streaks of blood we'd left along the spines; paper cuts and streams of sweat came with the job.

"Phone call," he yelled over the din. "Take it at my desk."

His nickname, Chrome Dome, served me well. I followed his shiny bald head to the tall platform in the center of the bindery and nervously climbed the steps. Only supervisors were allowed here. Who could be calling me?

At the top I was struck by the view: From one cinder-block wall to the other were skid-lined aisles and machines. Books were being sewn, glued, covered, and inspected. From this very spot, my boss scrutinized his employees like a priest scanning parishioners from a pulpit.

I picked up a black desk phone and felt the stares of my coworkers. When I heard Mom's voice, I was sure my cheeks turned two shades brighter.

"Grandma died this morning," she said efficiently, as if on a coffee break. "They couldn't revive her in the ambulance."

My tears fell easily. "How's Dad? I'll come home and—"

"There's nothing you can do here. Dad and Florian are still at the hospital. They'll get you at three, okay? We should be thankful Lucille had some time at home."

"But I don't think I can—"

"I'll see you later, Connie. I've got more calls to make."

The hands on the large wall clock formed a perfect right angle.

Quarter to twelve. I had a half-hour lunch and the rest of my shift to prepare myself. What could I possibly say to Dad and my uncle? Grandma had lived two miles away for nineteen years, yet I barely knew her. I drove her to the American Legion on Sunday to play cards, and we talked about the weather. After I took her back to the white clapboard on 2nd Street, she dug into her knitted coin purse and produced a Kennedy fifty-cent piece. I thanked her and left.

At 3:05, our gold Grand Prix parked across the street from the bindery. Why hadn't I told Mom I'd walk home? I envied my coworker Ann, her pigtails swinging as she cruised the sidewalk. I slipped between oncoming cars and saw the most important men in my life hunched like crows on a power line. Neither moved as I slid into the back. "I'm sorry," I said softly. Dad turned the key in the ignition. I noticed the deep creases on Florian's tanned face. Their eyes were fixed on the steamy concrete.

Our family sat in the front pew on the left side of the aisle for Grandma's service. Before us loomed St. John the Baptist himself, a larger-than-life ceramic with outstretched arms. Votives formed a bright picket fence around his bare feet. To our right, Grandma's glossy brown casket was draped with pink carnations.

This was my first funeral; I didn't know what to expect. Would Dad cry, as he had the night before at Grandma's showing? He had pulled a monogrammed handkerchief from the pocket of his suit jacket, removed his glasses, and sobbed loudly into the neat white square. I'd felt like a trespasser, watching from the doorway.

Now, as I clasped my hands in my lap, I realized I was silently praying. *Holy Mary, Mother of God, pray for us sinners now and at the hour of our death.* A shiver ran down my spine.

Father Watry, trim yet bent in the blackest of cassocks, entered the sanctuary and uttered the Latin invocation beginning the Mass. Even though he switched to English for our spoken responses, I felt like a stranger in the church of my childhood. We hadn't gone to Mass as a family. Mom attended the early service, the rest of us the late one. The wooden pews I'd polished as a fifth-grader were coldly unfamiliar.

Then Father swung the holy container of incense by its gold chain and blessed the casket. I thought of how he'd performed the same act by the crucifix on Good Friday two months earlier. First Jesus died. Then Grandma. Nothing could offer me comfort or lessen my fear of death. For me, there was no heaven or hell. People disappeared. One day, I would vanish, too.

After Father broke the bread and offered up the wine, we began our walk to the communion rail. We were similarly sorrowful, except Mom. If I touched her hard face, I was certain it would crack like a clay pot. She turned abruptly toward Bill, poked his arm, and hissed, "Not you. Not the way you look." He dropped down onto the pew, red-faced. His shoulder-length blond hair hung around his wire glasses like curtains on a picture window. I wanted to understand why he was obeying this time. How could Mom single him out, a mourner among other mourners? I patted his sports jacket, the navy one Dad had lent him. He didn't look up. When I passed his knees, I felt ashamed. My faith was on the brink of extinction in front of God, St. John the Baptist, and Grandma, lying just a few feet away, stone cold.

Mom was moved to the geriatric psych floor while her abdomen healed.

"She's the cream of the crop," Judy reported. "They won't release her until she starts eating. I tried grapes and chocolate chip cookies. Nothing. Hopefully the appetite stimulant will kick in."

"I can't believe she turned down cookies," I said.

"Her mind is active, though," Judy added. "She wondered what became of June Allyson. We were naming her movies, when she went into the bathroom, stared at the mirror, and said, 'I thought I was sixty-five!' Now *that* was sad. So I asked, 'What does that make me, with all this gray hair?'"

"She thinks she's younger," I echoed, "and yet can't recall losing Dad. How frustrating."

"Well, she hasn't forgotten her skin care and wants me to bring her a jar of Eterna. But get this: no wide-mouth jars in this joint, because someone might eat the contents."

"*What?*"

"That was my reaction until I heard the story of Mom rubbing toothpaste on her bottom."

I didn't know what to say. Everything was happening too fast.

"She's wearing a diaper, Con."

I felt a sudden hammering behind my eyes, a purplish-black knockout of the worst kind. The terror of my first migraine headache, when I was five years old, came back to me. Dad had insisted I nap after kindergarten. "But, Daddy," I'd cried. "I have lines in my head. Twirling, twirling lines, and there's just no end to them. Every time one gets all the way to the bottom, another begins at the top. Make them stop, Daddy."

"You're tired, honey," he'd answered. "No more complaints."

I'd lain on my pillow and shut my eyes. But there were the lines—neon green, then orange—and I'd followed them, over and over, until finally plunging into a dark, silent world.

By week's end, Mom nibbled on the snacks offered in the dayroom. Perhaps the doctor's admonition had hit home: Eat or die of dehydration. Judy's theory was equally plausible: Eat or face a nursing home. With food came the hope of a clearer mind.

"Mom wants to buy me a poodle," Judy quipped. "She's in a wheelchair, dangling her feet under a blanket, convinced she should go to Denver and pick one up."

"She never even liked your Samoyeds. And Denver? How on earth does she come up with this stuff?"

"Beats me. I told her I'd ask Terry. I didn't bother reminding her it's Bill who favors poodles."

Our mother was not a dog person—or an animal person, for that matter. If we managed to slip something through the back door on State Street, it usually got booted out fairly quickly. Laddie, an adorable beige puffball Dad bought at the pig fair, drove Mom crazy; she carted it off after four days. However, I never understood what happened while I was on my senior class trip to Washington, D.C. The morning I returned, my brother burst into my bedroom with a St. Bernard pup prancing behind him. I thought five consecutive sleepless nights had caused me to hallucinate.

"What the hell?" I said when Mom appeared, the former "I'll never tolerate another dog under this roof" person.

"Callie's drooling, Bill. Take her to the basement."

"In a minute. She hasn't met Connie."

I sat up, and Bill plopped Callie on my lap. Her fist-sized paws consumed the better part of my thighs. I rubbed her ears and her eyes met mine—the largest brown marbles I'd ever seen. I wondered how a St. Bernard would survive in our household.

Through June, Callie's appetite was enormous, and she gnawed everything in sight. She yanked me by the leash down 8th Street, swooping around the corner, and I stumbled behind. The chores were endless. Dad good-naturedly accepted the job of cleaning Callie's domain. I didn't think she'd last the fall. And I was right. She'd grown to my knees when Mom decided to call it quits. Dad agreed, but for different reasons. "She's too big to be cooped up. She needs the run of things."

Mom drove Callie to Rita and Don's. They were more than happy to adopt another member into their family. When I visited, Callie greeted me at the door on her hind legs, smashing her paws and tongue against the screen. I was relieved to see her free.

Judy's laugh broke my reverie. "Mom was so thrilled with her idea. She told the nurses I'd love a poodle as much as Bill loved Callie."

"Yet, a St. Bernard?"

"She had a soft spot for him, Con."

I thought about my brother, the angry yet brilliant middle child with so much expected of him: high grades, a college degree, and a respectable profession. He'd grown to be the strongest man in my life.

12

"She's sprung," Judy said tiredly on Saturday morning. "Those are Mom's words. Brighton Gardens wants another psych evaluation, however. And I've got to finish the guardianship papers. It's endless."

I closed my spiral notebook. My half-finished manuscript for a local poetry competition could wait, though recently, I'd clung to it like a life raft.

"Day to day, Jude. By the way, have you talked to Bill lately?"

"Thursday. He said to say hi to Mom. I'll be glad when her phone is connected."

I didn't have the heart to remind her that calls between Mom and Bill were irregular. Over the years, she had maintained a bitterness about his dropping in and out of college and wasting her and Dad's money in the process. Bill was tired of her incessant criticisms and grew weary of the fact that he couldn't meet her high standards. I wasn't sure their pattern of communication would change.

"For some reason," Judy added, "Mom's become very confessional. She apologized for treating Terry like a dog. She knows she never gave the poor guy a chance."

From the moment Mom met Judy's future husband, she disliked him intensely. Besides having long hair (although he kept it pony-tailed in her presence), he could never do the right thing. After a while, I didn't blame him for not trying; I knew all too well the personal cost of imperfection at the hands of my mother.

Mom, Judy, and Terry had spent the first Christmas after Dad died with us in California. One day, we'd decided to do some last-minute shopping while the kids were in school. When the van reached the bottom of the driveway, Mom glared at the cigarette butts lying end to end like dominoes in the gutter. "Terry, are those yours?" she asked sharply from the front seat.

"Yeah," he chuckled. "Connie can sweep them up."

I glanced at him in the rearview mirror; his wink confirmed my suspicion of an ill-timed joke.

"Do it yourself!" Mom yelled.

"Oh, Virginia. I'm just kidding."

It was too late. Mom's mood was cast in stone. Browsing became a chore, and she was mute during lunch. That evening, after I dressed for our annual trip to San Francisco, Mom announced she wasn't going.

"You'll miss the wreaths in Macy's windows," I protested. She changed into a thin nightgown, and we left without her.

"Virginia's still mad at me," Terry said. "I tried to be extra nice."

"Don't take it too personally," I answered sympathetically. "She's having a hard time. Their anniversary is the day after Christmas." It would have been Mom and Dad's fiftieth. When I'd mentioned it at breakfast, Mom had held the newspaper directly in front of her face and said, "I'm not discussing it. Not now, not ever." I felt as if I'd been swiped across the mouth.

At Union Square, Terry bought a dozen miniature yellow roses from a sidewalk vendor. "I'll make it up to her," he said. It was a generous gesture. However, Mom was one tough cookie; if she believed she'd been wronged, the grudge could last a lifetime.

When we arrived home, Terry offered her the bouquet. Bathrobed and groggy from dozing on the couch, Mom flicked her wrist, as if swatting a lake fly. I waited for Judy to come to his defense, but she didn't. I couldn't keep quiet. "Why can't you accept the flowers and say thank you? Honestly, you'd think he murdered someone."

Yet I knew why Mom had refused Terry's gift: She lacked graciousness, pure and simple. I realized her chances for a happy life were as slim as those of my reembracing the teachings of the Catholic Church.

When I was young, family outings were rare. When the carnival arrived at Bay Beach on the southern tip of Green Bay during the last, hot days of summer, we piled into the car with a picnic lunch and didn't return until supper.

We rode with the windows down, Mom less concerned with her hair than normal. Through Kimberly and Kaukauna, the breeze carried the rich smells of farmland: manure-fed fields and acres of sweet corn. Every mile filled me with anticipation; even being stuffed between the sweaty bodies of my siblings didn't dampen my excitement.

From a distance I spotted the curves of the bay, then the carnival tents like giant polka dots along the shore. As we got closer, they came to life with carousel horses, bumper cars, and spinning cages. Mom and Dad bought rolls of tickets. While Bill and Judy favored the bumper cars, I divided my tickets between the pony ride and the Ferris wheel. Atop a saddled chestnut, I was Annie Oakley, willing my mount to go faster and faster. But in a full day of clumping in circles, the pony merely kept a steady gait. I settled for being Dale Evans, humming into his hairy ears.

When the ride ended, I ran to the cherry seats of the Ferris wheel. I stretched my arms out to the sides of the car, and my blond braids swung in abandon. At the top of the sky I searched for my parents in the blur of sun-washed faces. Then I dropped and imagined Mom saying, "There she goes." It was better than heaven.

Sometimes I tried to picture them as children. I'd seen a few photographs: Dad, towheaded in knee-length britches and leather shoes. I wondered if he'd ridden a bicycle or swum in the river. I never thought to ask. And Mom, prim in a lace-collared dress and wavy bob. She said she'd felt like a prisoner in her house, tiptoeing on the second floor between the bedrooms of her depressed mother and the strange boarders they needed to take in from time to time. I felt sorry for Mom. Yet I was grateful she'd allowed laughter into her life, even if on only a handful of days, like those glorious ones at Bay Beach.

With each new residence, Mom seemed to reinvent herself. The initial move to Illinois sparked a thundering hostility. After her gallbladder operation, she drifted from confusion to submission. Now her return to Brighton Gardens revealed her craftiness as she devised ways to forge ahead.

"I'll go back to Wisconsin and find someone to live with," she told Judy.

"Not happening," Judy replied.

"Then I'll request a more suitable guardian." When pressed for names, Mom couldn't think of a soul.

I remembered the months after Dad's funeral. Mom regularly reported her activities, such as grocery shopping or trimming the evergreens. She'd ask, "Am I doing better?" I poured on the praise. "Definitely a more positive attitude." She explained that she didn't want to end up like her mother. Mom was the most resilient woman I knew; she'd survive under any circumstances.

"I take her for pizza and she eats like a packhorse," Judy said. "I'd better watch it, or I'll gain ten pounds." I was amazed by Mom's transformation from nearly starving herself to enjoying food again. Her disorientation waned, her mood mellowed, and our spirits were bolstered.

"And she's finally going down for music in the evenings. Nothing else, though—not even bingo."

"Mom's never been social," I said. "Did she ever belong to any group besides her card club? Christ, she didn't want *me* to do anything when I was a kid."

I recalled the thrill of second grade, running excitedly to the gym with Pam after school to hear about a new Brownie troop. I listened intently as the leader described art projects, Christmas caroling, and meetings at her home. However, Mom snuffed out any possibility. Girls marched through the hallways of St. John's in snappy skirts and matching vests, Brownie sashes displayed grandly across their chests. Exclusion hurt as much as my brother's pummeling.

My attempts to join the band in fifth grade were just as futile. "The *flute?*" Mom asked, scrunching her eyebrows. I never mentioned it again.

Yet I didn't want to be noticed in any way. When Sister chose me to play Mary in the Christmas pageant, I was mortified. Not only did I have to parade through the classroom in a deep-blue robe, I had lines to recite as well. Speaking was torture. All I needed was to sit at my desk and watch the world around me. I became an expert.

I begged my parents to send me to public school for seventh grade so I could be free of all past humiliations. I was shocked when they agreed. Within the brick walls of junior high, it was easy to go unnoticed in a crowd of adolescents. That is, until I was rediscovered.

"Connie is a capable student," my history teacher said to Mom during a conference. "But she doesn't raise her hand in class. I sense a rather deep shyness."

Mom answered, "I was thinking of enrolling her in ballet. An extracurricular activity might help."

This was news to me. Activities weren't as important to her as they were to me. Autumn turned into winter, and nothing more was said. I figured ballet had been a hoax all along, another dream just out of reach.

"Connie, I haven't been this happy in years," Mom chirped over the phone a few days after settling back into Brighton Gardens.

"Progress," I said, sinking into a leather chair in my bedroom.

"I think some of the men are looking at me. Joseph, the janitor, has taken to me and I to him."

I giggled. Mom's becoming involved with a man seemed as unlikely to me as flying to Paris for an extended vacation. I recalled her leaning against a kitchen counter on Palisades Lane while my father-in-law examined a faulty window. "Wood's warped," he said.

Mom looked him straight in the eye and cooed, "Oh, Al, you're so lucky to have such a beautiful family."

He sputtered and took a step back. "Just trying to help."

Now I was encouraged by the lilt in Mom's voice. Since she and Dad had had a solid relationship, perhaps her flirtatiousness and the satisfaction she received from the attention of other men filled a void for her now. I welcomed Mom's taking an interest in anything, or, in this case, anyone.

Her spirits kept rising. She told me her teddy bears fit neatly on her rocker. She'd met a lady at dinner, and the woman in the room next to hers owned a Yorkie. I eagerly grabbed every thread of this unforeseen joyful energy, knowing it could snap at any time.

As a child, I was convinced my mother and father loved each other. Not in a show-off, mushy way, like couples I'd seen on television. After working eight hours, Ward Cleaver came through the front door and headed straight for June, usually aproned beside a hot oven. He'd peck her cheek and they'd beam, radiant as if parted for weeks. Later, after a hearty meal, they'd read side by side on the sofa, Ward with a book and June with *Good Housekeeping*. Occasionally, their shoulders touched.

My parents didn't openly hug, kiss, or greet each other kindly. It seemed as if it were too much effort to say, "Hi, dear. How was your day?" They were connected, like a loyal team of horses to a plow, by three children and duty, by sacrifice and hard work. But in the evening, no matter how many harsh words had been spoken or doors had been slammed, they retreated to their bedroom together.

Every June they rented a cottage for one week on Shawano Lake. Although only an hour away, it made us feel as if we'd entered another world. Sunshine streamed through birch along the highway, then washed the alabaster siding of the tiny house I loved. I'd be the first one out of the Ford to see if anything had changed. I took comfort in the army-green metal chairs facing the shore, the kind with shell-shaped backs that rocked ever so slightly. Water lapped the wood dock, and I ran to it like a sprinter to the finish line. It took all I had not to jump in with my clothes on.

Days on the lake were long and lazy. My siblings and I swam after breakfast, lunch, and sometimes supper. I relished cold water on my scalp, free from the mandatory rubber cap of the city pool. I was a competent swimmer and practiced the difficult backstroke diligently. At night, under a single, dusty ceiling bulb, we played board games on the floor of the wide screened porch. Even Mom seemed relaxed, oblivious to the sand we'd traipsed in.

I was allowed to bring Pam the summer after sixth grade. *Thank God,* I thought, since Bill was moodier than ever and Judy's boyfriends tended to follow her everywhere. Pam and I explored the lake. We rowed a paint-chipped boat among the lily pads, searching for driftwood. In shallow parts cliques of minnows scurried with each slap of our oars.

One afternoon we walked the edge of the highway to the general store for souvenirs. Pam bought a varnished rectangular box that smelled like our cedar closet at home. I'd saved my allowance for a porcelain tabby and a gold chain with a cross. I couldn't wait to wear it at dinner.

We hurried back to the cottage, bathed, and excitedly pulled on the sundresses we'd packed for eating out. A restaurant was a treat compared with our occasional Friday fish fry: cloth napkins instead of paper; tall, frosted glasses of Coca-Cola, not the short plastic ones that usually bore traces of old lipstick. As we stood in front of the bathroom mirror, me clasping my necklace and Pam brushing her towel-dried hair, voices exploded from my parents' room. Mortified, I shut the door. Pam bent over at the waist and worked more vigorously. *How could they ruin everything?* blared in my head. Pam's parents would never have done that. When I'd gone with them to their cottage in Antigo, it had drizzled most of the week, yet the mood had been cheerful. Even when we'd driven to the dump after dark and watched black bears feast on garbage, her family had been content. I'd felt safe huddled in the station wagon with Pam.

No one noticed my necklace when I slid across the vinyl car seat beside Pam and Dad. Once Judy, Bill, and Mom closed the back doors, Dad started the ignition and yanked the stick shift into reverse. Gravel flew in every direction.

"You idiot!" Mom yelled. "Go on. Show them what a fool you are." Her words sizzled in the humid air like power lines in an electrical storm. Pam and I leaned on each other as the car went faster and faster. I was sure we were holding our breath. There was another time he'd been reckless behind the wheel—on Highway 57 to Green Bay, to visit Judy—when I'd realized he'd been drinking. As he carelessly passed other cars on the two-lane road, I prayed we wouldn't end up in a ditch or plastered to the hood of an oncoming truck.

Now we walked single file to our appointed table in the restaurant.

My insides quaked at the thought of eating. I wanted to run back into the open light of day, far from the scene I knew would unfold. And, sure enough, Mom criticized the food and the ineptness of the waitress. Dad rolled his eyes, then ate with his head down. Once or twice a remark was slung in his direction, but he ignored her, swallowing bread and potatoes and beer, until he'd had enough of everything. Before the rest of us finished, Dad left the table. We found him later, snoozing in the front seat of the car. I envied his ability to block it all out. I'd be apologizing to Pam for weeks in my dreams.

13

I pressed "save" on my laptop, and "Virginia's Inventory" faded into my screen saver of the Canadian Rockies. I welcomed its neutrality of earth and sky; after three days of going through Mom's things, I was drained. Although Judy and I had agreed to work in the garage last because it was the least encumbered space, it was clearly no easier.

I leaned on Grandma's Bendix and cried. Judy wrapped her arms around me, and I appreciated her empathy. We'd learned this tenderness of touch and affection as adults. How useful it would have been when we were younger, in a household devoid of outward expression. I don't recall receiving an embrace for a handmade birthday present, a pat on the back for a good report card, or an "I love you." Encouragement and praise were doled out in meager proportions. We survived a different way: individually, silently. It was a lonely world.

Upon waking one October morning during my sophomore year in college, I felt the newness of a ring on my left hand. I'd accepted the square diamond from Gary the night before in Riverside Park. Although an unusual calm and ten hours of delicious sleep filled me completely, I wondered how I'd tell my parents. They'd always approved of Gary, ever since I'd met him at a winter dance before I'd turned sixteen. He'd stood on the opposite side of St. Pat's gym, arms crossed and legs planted two feet apart, and eyes aimed directly at me from beneath a mound of dark brown hair. In an instant, I felt like a woman.

I heard a tap on my bedroom door, and Mom breezed in, cheerfully announcing we'd leave for the store in an hour. I remained motionless beneath the sheets. She smiled suspiciously and with one swoop uncovered everything I thought I could hide. "I knew it. I just knew it!" she bellowed. "Ed, Connie has a surprise for you!"

I wobbled into the kitchen, nervous about my current status and independence. Their reactions were mismatched. Mom grinned obnoxiously. Dad was somber, clearly processing the news before speaking. As he plugged in the percolator and measured the Folgers, I couldn't imagine anything lonelier than my leaning against the counter on the other end of the room.

"You have my blessing," he said, while retrieving a spoon from the silverware drawer.

"Of course, you'll stay in school," Mom chimed in eagerly, already planning the next few years of my life.

I waited for something else to happen, an opening of arms into which I longed to run. But it was business as usual: Saturday breakfast of bacon and eggs.

The following August, a few hours before the five o'clock candlelight service, Mom stood behind me as I set my hair in rollers in front of the bathroom mirror. "Don't wear your glasses for the wedding," she said. "You look prettier without them."

I laughed carelessly, until I saw her face—dead serious, with an air of self-importance. My shock, a mix of humiliation and anger, shot out from my gold wire frames.

"That's ridiculous! I'll trip down the aisle."

"I doubt that. Dad will have your arm."

I briskly turned around. "God, Mom. I want to see my wedding and my guests. Go do what you need to do, and leave me alone."

She left in a huff, muttering about my selfishness, then my brother's, since he hadn't returned yet from swimming. I'd been wrong to think that I could succeed in breaking down Mom's resistance to conveying outward signs of love and emotion. The tender mother-daughter moment I'd imagined had evaporated.

Bill finally blew in, and I relinquished the bathroom to him. He didn't apologize for being late, and he offered no words of congratulation or support.

I felt extremely alone while powdering my cheeks and applying mascara in my bedroom. Then Mom came in and slipped my wedding gown over my head, zipped it, and pulled me to the gilded oval mirror at the end of the hallway. "Stand right here." She placed the veil on my long hair. "Let's take the first picture, side by side, glancing into the mirror. Without your glasses." Before I could respond, she'd scurried to the living room to retrieve the photographer. I posed and accepted our relationship for what it was: flawed and frustrating, yet uniquely intertwined like the yellow and mint carnations I'd carry down the aisle.

Mom had a label for everyone. While Judy was creative and Bill was smart, I was pretty. I was resigned to being nonartistic and content with my intellectual status. But I never regarded myself as pretty. I had a large nose with a bump on its bridge. No one said it was broken that first time, but I knew the moment my bike slammed into the telephone pole on the corner of State and 9th Streets, igniting the most spectacular fireworks in my head. When I woke the next morning, Mom said I was a sight to behold with two black eyes.

Over time, my nose became a reliable source of embarrassment. Yet Mom was insistent on categorizing me as "the pretty one." When a friend didn't choose me as a bridesmaid, Mom concocted a theory: "She thinks you'll show her up." I reasoned that the bridesmaids she had selected were more outgoing and fun. By then, my so-called shyness had turned into social ineptness. I was fearful of groups; interacting in nearly any situation made my stomach flutter.

With our inventory complete, Judy and I surveyed Mom's dining room table and the items that would eventually find their way into our own homes. On my designated half, an Osterizer blender for Ryan, a wind-up doll for Cara, cookie cutters, an antique eggbeater, and a pewter-framed wedding photograph of my parents. In a corner stood the scuffed bookcase of Bill's childhood. I remembered how he smoothed tinfoil tightly across the top, placed a statue of the Virgin Mary in the center, and positioned adoring angels and ivory votives around her. My siblings and I knelt before his shiny altar, Mary's naked feet at my eye level. The fact that Mom had saved the bookcase was surprising. Although Bill claimed indifference, I couldn't part with it. I'd ship it to my home by way of UPS with the other keepsakes.

I recalled the last time I'd felt such remorse here, seven years earlier, after Dad died. I'd taken Amtrak to Naperville, then driven up with Judy. It was October. Our parents' usually immaculate yard was coated with the downed, soggy leaves of a recent rain. The evergreens drooped from summer's growth. Yet when we entered the house, I understood. It looked as though it had been cleaned from top to bottom. There wasn't a dirty dish in the orange double sink or so much as a scrap of paper on the countertop. The dining room table gleamed, as did the artificial-fruit bowl in its center. Even Mom appeared fresh and tidy in a cotton blouse and khakis.

"Bring your stuff." She motioned toward the guest room. "I'll show you Dad's closet."

Mom slid a dark paneled door on its track. "All to Goodwill," she said. "Except some shirts I gave Don. Judy, I thought you'd like Dad's gray sweatshirt. His camel sports jacket is for you, Connie."

I was shocked by the emptiness. I reached for the lone item hanging on the rod and saw Dad, standing by his suitcase outside the United terminal at the Oakland airport. When most men traveled in casual attire, Dad donned his camel jacket and brown corduroy slacks, which made him clearly recognizable from the front seat of my van. Now I raised a sleeve of the wool blend to my face and detected a faint reminder of the cigars he'd been forced to give up. I was chilled.

"Is there anything else?" I asked.

"The fleece blanket for Cara," Mom said, pointing to a plastic bag on the shelf.

"That's yours, not Dad's." I sounded more impatient than I wanted.

"Look around; I don't care," she said on her way out. "I'll start lunch."

Judy sat on the paisley bed beside me. When she finally spoke, it was with an air of indignation. "He was our father. Her husband, but *our* father."

I knew what she meant. Mom insisted no one understood what she was going through. We comforted her as best we could and waited for solace in return. It never came. Not once did she voice motherly concern for our feelings. Not one loving word for our loss. Dad's death was hers and hers alone.

Even my brother, ill upon his arrival from Florida, was similarly disregarded. "You deal with him," Mom told us after Bill vomited on her bedroom carpet. "I've had enough sickness." So we did, eventually driving him to the emergency room the night before Dad's funeral. We took turns holding a plastic bowl under his chin while he heaved. When we couldn't stomach anymore, we waited outside the curtain and shook our heads at his scheduled appendectomy. I realized then what Mom had gone through. She'd nursed Dad at home to the very end: changed sweat-soaked sheets, prepared food that wasn't eaten, and doled out pills every hour of every day. How much could one person take?

The following morning was damp and especially gray, the type of weather I hadn't missed since I'd moved to California twenty years before. The black skirt I'd packed seemed flimsy and inappropriate, but with no alternative, I dressed, knowing I'd be chilly. Ryan and Cara got ready more quickly than normal, no doubt sensing the hurriedness in their grandmother's voice. As she scurried about, giving instructions for the toaster and opinions regarding the bad timing of Bill's operation, I was sure sleep deprivation added to her nervousness.

"Do these slacks look too short, Connie? I think Mrs. Scovy cut off more than she should have." Mom smoothed the navy blue linen along her hips with several flourishes of her fingers. "What about this pin on my blouse? Too fancy?"

I glanced at the round pearl on the burgundy silk, puzzled by the rare question regarding her attire. "It's lovely," I answered, patting her shoulder. "Now slow down and breathe." She closed her eyes momentarily and exhaled a peppermint huff of Listerine.

The main sitting room of the mortuary reminded me of a spread in *Architectural Digest:* brightly lit and exceedingly spare. Flowered wingback chairs were precisely grouped. Ivory-shaded lamps on cherry end tables cast an elegant glow. Ryan and Cara slumped into a corner love seat, wary of accidentally spotting their grandfather.

All morning they'd insisted that they didn't want to see another dead person. It had been only a year since a boy on Ryan's soccer team had died. When Gary had taken Ryan and Cara to the boy's funeral, at the Catholic church, they hadn't been prepared for the open casket. Cara had been traumatized: For weeks afterward, she had demanded that the lights remain on at bedtime, and she had checked on me several times during each night.

Now I was grateful when my in-laws settled next to them. Mom, Gary and I, and Judy and Terry hung up our coats and waited for the mortician to appear. Even though I knew Dad was lying in the adjoining room with its door slightly ajar, I wanted to put off the inevitable for as long as possible.

The mortician was younger than I'd expected, yet obviously seasoned in his profession. My knees shook beneath the hemline of my skirt as he explained the thirty-minute viewing before he'd close the casket and begin the service. It all seemed terribly wrong. How could I do what I needed beside the body of my father in half an hour? That was how long it took to water the lawn or bake a cake, a mere speck of time compared with the enormity of his passing. My chest felt crushed.

I took Gary's arm. At the side of the rented casket, Mom said, "It doesn't even look like Ed, with that hair!" She tearfully turned and left the room. I was appalled to see that Dad's thick white hair, the constant during his struggle with cancer, had been tinted the shade of my copper boiler.

I kissed his hands, which had been crossed on his chest, then tucked a note card under the lapel of his good brown suit. The words I'd written on the train through Colorado were overwhelming. "Gaze peacefully at the season's brilliant beauty, and gracefully cast your line again." Fishermen knee-deep in an ancient river had reminded me of Dad.

I understood now, more than ever, how time transformed everything. And change, with all its beginnings and endings, never failed to frighten me.

St. John's Cemetery curved along Highway P, a half mile from Mom and Dad's home. Ever since I was a girl, I'd accompanied Dad to honor the memory of his father, mother, and brother. Now, on a raw, gloomy morning, we'd bury his cremated remains as well.

Gary parked the rental car behind Judy's station wagon. I glanced at the familiar tombstones. Some families were clustered together, while other, less fortunate individuals had entered eternity in stark isolation. I thought of my apprehensive children in the backseat and felt blessed.

Judy had explained the arrangements to Bill the day before, as he had lain drugged after his surgery. "We meet the mortician at eleven," she'd begun awkwardly, biting her lower lip. "He'll bring the ashes in the urn Mom picked out." Judy looked at her for approval. Mom, still in her funeral attire, stared listlessly out the window.

"We're also buying three roses to place on Dad's grave. One from each grandchild."

"Thank you," Bill said softly, his eyes watering behind wire frames that hung loosely on his noticeably thinner face. "From me and Brian."

I'd felt sorry for them both: my four-year-old nephew in Florida, who'd never experience his grandfather's wit; and Bill, who'd mourn privately and by himself in St. Elizabeth's.

Now we joined the humble assemblage on the grass. I was somewhat startled by the helium balloons Judy and Mom held in their gloved hands. In the hurry of the morning, I'd forgotten Mom's idea of releasing them at the end of our farewell. Judy untangled the strings of our requested colors: blue, red, yellow, and Cara's favorite, lavender. I took Cara's hand and, with Gary and Ryan close behind, carefully stepped across the spongy earth until my grandparents' granite marker came into view.

I flipped up my collar, turned, and saw the mortician and my in-laws walking toward us. They could have been old friends, chatting, their wool coats only inches apart. I was struck by how life's rituals make one family out of many.

There was a freshly dug spot to the right of the headstone. The mortician placed a brass container on the plywood that covered it and said, "Take as long as you need." I stared at the urn, holding all that was left of my father. Seventy-three years of doing the best you can with the little you have. I glanced tenderly at Mom, stoop-shouldered and old. She'd join him one day in the oblong piece of ground no larger than a sandbox.

Two months after we moved Mom to Illinois, our attorney finished the guardianship papers. Mom agreed there was no reason to hold on to the house.

"I know I'll live here for the rest of my life," she said into the phone after returning from a Fourth of July parade with Judy.

"You'll finally have family around," I said. Although Rita and Don had lived close by, she had never regarded them as family. I wasn't sure why. We were it. No matter how earnestly I'd tried to convince her otherwise, she stuck to her belief like a moth to flame, burning ties with each passing year.

"Yes, Judy works so hard . . . I don't know where I'd be if it wasn't for her."

I wanted to say, *By me, in California*, but I wasn't about to begrudge my sister her goodwill and growing affection for our mother. Theirs was a relationship just beginning to blossom.

For most of my life, Mom and I seemed to play our own version of tug-of-war. She'd say dry the dishes, and I'd do it without balking. I knew when to speak. If she shaped pancake batter on the griddle to form apples or pears, humming in the process, I caught on to her good mood. If she flipped and slapped them hard, I kept quiet.

But I finally grew tired of obeying her every command and constantly watching for her moods to change. I took a stand in the fourth grade. I'd had enough of tight braids held together by rubber bands and announced bravely, "I'm cutting my hair."

Mom's eyelids snapped open like thin shades. "You'll be sorry," she said.

"I'm old enough," I answered.

"Suit yourself."

I felt quite grown-up and sophisticated with my newfound power.

Mom drove me to her beauty parlor downtown. Her stylist asked, "Are you sure?" I pointed to the bottom of my earlobe and said, "To here, please." I wanted to look like Hayley Mills in *The Parent Trap*.

As if I were a regular customer, Sandy wrapped a ribbon of white tissue around my neck and flung a black drape across my shoulders. I almost giggled at my nun-like appearance in the mirror, until I saw Mom's solemn face above mine. "Oh my God," she stuttered as Sandy raised her scissors. When she placed an eight-inch sheath on my lap, I regarded it as a souvenir, a remembrance of my first crack at freedom. It had been worth every lustrous golden inch.

When I was older, after Judy and Bill left for college, Mom almost glowed with her lightened responsibilities. If Dad worked the late shift, suppers were simple. I'd eat a tuna sandwich in front of NBC's *Nightly News* while she sat on the step stool in the kitchen with the *Post Crescent* sprawled across the countertop. But by Saturday, Mom always became hurried and tense about cleaning and laundry, and her calm demeanor vanished. It was nearly impossible to stay out of her way in our small house.

One night we had an argument. Even though time has erased the subject on which we differed, I still recall its outcome—a sharp slap across my cheek that made me hate her. "Feel better now?" I asked boldly.

Her face flushed, as it had when she'd miscalculated her time in front of the sunlamp. She mumbled under her breath and retreated down the hallway. "I didn't think so," I said triumphantly, closing my door on her and on our spotless house.

"Connie, I never thought I'd have fun again," Mom continued. "There were marching bands and horses decked out in red, white, and blue. Maybe this is the person I've been inside all these years."

Antidepressants had clearly stabilized her mood. It saddened me that the potential for happiness had so often eluded her. Life had been one long, unending struggle. Now I couldn't imagine anything more terrifying for Mom than losing her mind, especially since she knew it was slipping away little by little, like evening light in autumn. I viewed it as the battle of her life; after wrinkles and liver spots, she regarded it as the ultimate degradation.

"I signed the listing papers today," Judy said cheerfully. "Subject to court approval, but Craig doesn't expect a holdup. He recommended a realtor—my friend Pat from high school. She sold a ranch in the neighborhood. She scheduled an open house for Saturday."

I was leery of strangers plodding through Mom's home. *Oh, look, Alan,* I imagined an eager young wife saying to her husband. *A fireplace and new curtains.* Then her hopes would be dashed upon entering the kitchen: *No dishwasher or disposal!* I preferred to picture an older, retired couple falling in love with the place, content with my mother's decorating quirks.

"But we've got a more immediate issue, Con. Mom has only one bra."

"How did that happen?" I asked, considering the disconcerting possibilities.

"The home does the laundry, so I'll bet another old lady is wearing Mom's battered underwear."

I laughed lightly. "What about Mom?"

"She claims she washes her bra every night, although she's not entirely sure. I'm taking over laundry duties."

"You don't have to," I said.

"I know, but she asked me." The exhaustion in Judy's voice was palpable. She didn't need any more to do. But she pressed on. "Anyway, we've got bigger problems. Mom complains about everyone: They're mean; they pee on the living-room chairs. She's threatened to walk out the door and down the highway. I said I'd better buy her a bright orange jacket so she doesn't get run over."

I recalled a conversation I'd had with Mom after a friend of hers lost her five-year-old daughter to leukemia. Before she died, she told Jane she saw angels dressed in shimmering gowns. Jane said it was a source of comfort. "I don't think I could bear it," Mom said.

"You'd find a way," I answered.

14

"This isn't what you'd call luxury living," Mom said when I phoned the Saturday morning of the open house. "It's boredom city, except when someone dies."

I sighed. "Why not ask the guy you met last week to go for a walk? What's his name? Al?"

"He thinks I'm a very nice woman. Classy, not like the other bags. A dope picked her nose at the breakfast table and hid it in a napkin. I reported her, you know."

"Have some patience, Mom. Sometimes you've got to look the other way."

"I can't stand these people! There's a picnic this afternoon, but I'm not going."

"Perhaps that's just what you need. Fresh air can do wonders." In this case, I knew I was dead wrong. Nothing would cheer her. Not even me. Yet I'd selfishly yearned to hear her voice; Judy and I hadn't told her about the open house. And because her dementia was progressing, Mom didn't always remember her home. The burden of our secret was suffocating.

There were so many things I never told my mother. As a terrified first grader, how could I answer "What did you learn today?" with the absolute truth? The story hadn't passed my lips when I'd turned sideways at my desk to admire the haloed Virgin in a frame on the wall, heard the dreaded clacking of Sister Tolentine's angry beads and the swish of her habit, then felt her cold, dry hand across my neck with a force that nearly sent me flying. "Sit straight in your chair," her man-voice roared. I did, my skin aflame with humiliation.

And I hadn't revealed the real reason behind my desperation to leave St. John's for the public junior high. His name was Pete. He was dark complected and the shortest boy in our sixth-grade class. When we marched single file to the coatroom at recess and lunch, he would be waiting by my hook with a toothy, ratlike grin. I'd try to grab my jacket, and *wham*—a squared fist just beneath my ribs. I'd double over while he sauntered away, a puffed-up rooster ready to crow.

I was too afraid of Pete to tattle to our lay teacher, although she was genuinely kind. It was easier to plan my escape: lie to my parents by saying the nuns were too mean, and leave the familiar and my friends, rather than return for more punishment in the seventh grade. Besides, even those friends had failed me. Girls who'd clutched jackets to their own chests in the coatroom. Boys oblivious to anything other than their next game of playground ball. A cowardly cloud hung over so many young Roman Catholic heads.

I told no one except for gruff Father Joe in a dreary confessional, and even that was a filtered version. "Bless me, Father, for I have sinned. . . . I've hated another at least ten times." He pronounced my penance and banged down the wood window. I was forgiven.

When I was older, I said to Mom, "I want to tell you something about my childhood." She rested her iron alongside a handkerchief and asked almost smugly, "You weren't sexually abused, were you?"

I was stunned by her callousness. "No, nothing like that." Had she really considered it a possibility? And by whom? Her question made me feel as if I'd been unprotected all along, as if the adults in my life could have turned the other cheek. When she resumed ironing with the proficiency of a short-order cook, I nailed the lid on my secret. The truth was more trouble than it was worth.

"We got an offer," Judy nearly warbled the next week.

"Already?" I said. "How much? Who?"

"A young woman from South Dakota. Her dad owns a restaurant in town. The deal sounds promising, but Pat wants to counter."

I pictured myself driving through the Palisades in a year. I'd spot an unfamiliar car parked in Mom's driveway, maybe a Mustang or a Civic, something consistent with the lifestyle of a single person. I'd resist the urge to peek through its filmed windows.

"Great news, Jude. When are you going to tell her?"

"I did last night. I figured she'd make a scene, but all she said was, '$127,500? I put the value at $145. Oh well.'"

"That's it?"

"She got really anxious. Couldn't figure out the scar on her abdomen until I said 'gallbladder operation.' Then she repeated the same old stories from Christmas."

Sundowners, I thought. By six o'clock in the evening, dementia often struck another blow.

"And she raved about Al. He reminds her of a friend in Wisconsin, six-foot and lanky. The aides and I think she's happy *only* when a man's around."

"What is it about Mom and men all of a sudden?"

Judy laughed. "Who knows? You haven't heard the best part yet."

I settled into a chaise lounge on the back porch. As a hummingbird whizzed from one purple azalea to the next in search of life-sustaining nectar, I realized Mom had been doing just that—grasping for a way to survive in Brighton Gardens.

Judy's voice softened. "Mom wonders if she's being disloyal to Dad. I said, 'If you want a relationship, that's fine. He's been gone seven years.' Mom said, 'What have I been doing for seven years? I complained too much, didn't I?' Honestly, Con, I almost died from laughing."

"Why couldn't she come clean forty years ago? Could have saved a lot of heartache."

For some reason, I always felt the tug of childhood. Not a gentle pull, but more of a sudden yank, like I'd felt in my armpit when I was whirled across the ice rink during the frenzy of Crack the Whip. Now the same scenes appeared and disappeared in random blurs.

I saw Mom and me shopping at the grocery store on 5th Street. She studied the cuts of meat in a display case as if contemplating a new car. After the butcher sliced the ham she finally chose, she said, "Oh, I don't like the looks of *that*. Is it fresh?" The serious man in his bloodied apron assured her it was. Mom dismissed him with a wave of her hand, then complained loudly all the way to frozen foods. I wanted to tell her to be quiet, that no one cared about the stupid ham, and, worse still, about how embarrassed I was. But I didn't have the guts and headed down the bakery aisle instead.

I heard Mom as we searched for Dad's undershirts at Jandry's. "Why is there never a clerk around when you need one? Doesn't anyone work here?" Her words carried through the men's department like a screech owl's lament over the backyard at twilight. Within seconds, a puzzled woman appeared and I hid behind a rack of bathrobes.

When the streetlights blinked on and night air swirled over the oleanders and my bare legs, I snuck into the house. I quietly closed the bedroom's double doors so as not to disturb Gary's movie. "What is Mom *really* worried about?"

"What you and Bill will think of Al. She's so against the roommate idea that she's considering Al for the second bedroom of her suite."

"Wow, that's fast," I said. Glancing at the lemon dab of moon beyond my blinds, I wondered if life would ever feel normal. I was sure Mom felt the same. "What did you say?"

"To wait at least another week. I'm hesitant to cross her, since the interview is coming up. If she claims she's not happy at Brighton Gardens, the judge could appoint an attorney to fight us."

"Well, Jude, maybe she'll change her mind tomorrow." I couldn't picture Mom living with anyone else, especially a man. Yet after years of scant socializing and isolation, a boyfriend, lawyers, social workers, and health care professionals breezed in and out of her life like flies at a barbecue. At this point, anything was possible.

Sometimes I daydreamed about what Mom's life would have been like if she hadn't married or had children. My grandfather's four sisters never did; two became Notre Dame nuns, and two remained single, passing away in their nineties.

I didn't think Mom would age as graciously. I pictured her in a cottage on the Fox River. After managing the stenographic department, she'd return to a solitary supper of split-pea soup. She'd share stories with coworkers and visit family on obligatory holidays. Her dreams would be minimal and close to home—a decent pay raise, a modern sofa. She'd decline any suggestion of travel. She'd buy a Siamese cat to ward off loneliness. Yes, I was certain Mom could do quite nicely without us.

She proved me wrong the November after Ryan turned two. Gary and I had agreed that moving to California would be the best choice for his career and our tight finances. I said, "You call my parents; I don't think I can." So he did, explaining he'd be leaving in a week and I'd stay behind with Ryan to sell our condo.

Within seconds, his jaw dropped and his face paled. He held the phone limply in his hand and said, "They hung up on me."

I heard from Mom three weeks later, after Gary started his new job in Walnut Creek, a countrified name for a bedroom community of San Francisco. "Will you be living in this 'Walnut Creek'?" she asked, as I divided clothes between suitcases and bags for Goodwill.

"No, Pleasant Hill," I answered.

"Whatever," she said. "When will I get to see our little guy? You've hurt us more than you know."

"I'm sorry," I said, holding back a torrent of tears. This guilt was worse than anything; she needed us after all. And although I needed a mother, she stayed away until we hugged good-bye. When Gary and I drove our Honda down Highway 41, with Ryan bundled and buckled in his car seat, I nearly floated on the heavy carpet of clouds, satisfied with being invisible. This time Mom would have to adapt to my life, with all its confusing and disappointing decisions.

Judy and I questioned ourselves constantly about whether we were making the right choices for Mom's care. Relatives were supportive, friends encouraging. Yet we battled an inferno, fueled by court deadlines, living arrangements, and Mom's steady decline. I was sadly aware of Judy alone on the front lines, riding the ever-changing winds of despair.

Although I was grateful Dad couldn't bear witness, I wondered how he'd view our efforts. I imagined him in a striped polo, rocking Miffy on his lap. "Just go with the flow, Virginia. The girls have your best interests at heart." She'd bristle: "I wouldn't be so sure, mister." I pictured myself there, too, asking impatiently, "Can't you just trust us?" I wanted it to be that simple.

It was comforting now to remember Dad. I saw him stretched out on Cara's bedroom floor for a game of Memory. As he peeked slyly under a corner of an animal picture, she scolded, "Grandpa, you're cheating again."

"I'm the naughtiest kid on the block," he answered, and Cara tumbled on the carpet beside him, hysterical with the inconceivable notion. "Sometimes I am, too," she confessed. "Well, then," Dad said, "us blondies have to stick together." She'd squeal, "But, Grandpa, your hair is gray!" Together they'd roar, the game completely forgotten.

Now I felt like the naughtiest kid on the block, for not figuring out Mom's condition until her world blew sky high. If only she hadn't been her normally contentious self. If only I had understood the signs and been bold enough to confront her.

The attorney who interviewed Mom agreed Brighton Gardens was an appropriate placement.

"Mom admits she has nowhere else to go," Judy said. "And she wants me to remain her guardian. But she's worried about Al moving in. What if they don't get along?"

"Like you said, let's wait it out. Each day brings such new excitement."

"Right," Judy laughed, "but always over old issues. Like the house. Mom asked to see it before the auction. She thought she could help us pack."

I cringed. "Let's see. A four-hour drive to somewhere she has trouble remembering. Anxiety, panic attacks, unexpected diarrhea . . . There's no way we could handle her, Jude. We'd all be nuts."

I felt ashamed to utter the basic truth, but just as obligated to protect us. After all, as Mom frequently asked Judy, "Who else is going to watch over me?"

15

"**B**ad news, Con," Judy reported a couple of weeks before my second visit and the inventory. "Mom's getting a roommate."

"Damn, not now."

"So she has two concerns: sharing a bathroom, and lack of privacy when Al drops by."

"When's it happening?"

"Soon. Also, Pat checked on Mom's house. The screens on the master bedroom had been pried."

"Man, what else can go wrong?" I tapped my teak desk several times so as not to be jinxed. Our conversation, like so many others over the months, was exhausting.

"Well, at least Mom's agreed that traveling to Wisconsin is a bad idea." I heard a sense of relief in Judy's voice.

"Thank God. Why the change of heart?"

"Your guess is as good as mine, Con. The skin color of the aides doesn't bother her anymore, either. As Mom loves to say, 'You can't tell by me.'"

I didn't know anyone else who uttered that phrase. It seemed to be sort of an admission on Mom's part that she wasn't as knowledgeable as she portrayed herself to be. Now Judy didn't understand Mom's letting go of her lifelong prejudices, and neither did I. What I wouldn't have given for a rational discussion with Mom. To learn the whys and how comes that were as elusive as the deer beyond my backyard fence during the heat of the day. At least I knew they'd return when the sun dropped behind the hill. I couldn't be certain of anything regarding my mother.

I awoke drenched in sweat, staring straight up, where the ceiling fan steadily churned the night air. As I unwound the sheet tangled between my thighs, I still plodded down the disquieting halls of high school, passing room after unfamiliar room. The recurring nightmare had barely changed over the summer. Perhaps a rumpled Mr. Day replaced the neatly coiffed Miss Olsen at the blackboard. The sensation upon waking, however, never varied. I was miserably lost and alone. Maybe this was how Mom felt. I checked my alarm clock: 1:30 am. I wouldn't wake Gary.

I settled on the sofa with the TV remote and clicked to a movie channel to avoid the deafening intrusion of commercials. Even *A River Runs Through It,* about two brothers enraptured by fly-fishing in the abundant rivers of Montana, couldn't distract me. I realized I'd met my greatest fear head-on—that of losing my mind. As Mom regressed, as had her father's sister, the possibility was extremely real.

Earlier in the week, I'd gone to the mall to buy her a nightgown. Less than an hour had passed between my parking and choosing a generic, knee-length dusty rose that would be the least objectionable. Yet there I stood on the curb outside Penney's, scrunching my eyebrows and thinking, *Where is my car?* I closed my eyes and concentrated. Yes, I'd locked the door and thrown my purse over my shoulder. I'd sideswiped a wad of gum, nearly twisting my ankle on a dip in the concrete. I'd heard the wind, noticed the trees brushing the sky. Of course. I'd parked near an embankment of pines on the left side of the lot.

Now I wondered what else I'd forget, if I would lose the larger, more significant things in life, as Mom had. She didn't remember her parents, her wedding day, or the home she shared in the Palisades with Dad. Even he was fading from view. I recoiled at the very thought of her forgetting me as well.

On a clear day, Mom was absolutely aware that her memories were being plucked from her brain like feathers from a chicken. I couldn't imagine the horror. I couldn't imagine surviving without everything

I'd learned or read, without the pictures of my family, my children. Where would I live? Whom would I know? When, just when, would this start happening to me?

"So, as it turns out," Judy announced the evening before my flight, "Al's a drinking man."

"Oh?" I said, adopting the tone Judy had perfected: a long *o*, followed by another syllable of disbelief.

"Mom complains that he carries a flask of whiskey. At the restaurant last night, he ordered a couple Manhattans."

"Has she gotten on his case yet?"

"Oh, she's steaming. I don't think she'll stay interested in a man too attached to a bottle."

Why not? She'd had plenty of practice. Even though she'd cursed the money Dad wasted in taverns, Mom had never left the house in anger. "In those days, wives didn't just pack up and leave," she'd often explained. "You stuck it out because it was expected. How would you feel if I'd broken up our family?" As a loyal daughter, I thought it was a topic better left undiscussed. But as a grown woman with children of my own, I'd grappled with the complexity of her life. What would I have done in her narrow, size 7 shoes? Stood my ground like a pigeon in a storm, claws clamped and wings tucked tight, braced for the unknown? Or thrown in the towel, claimed what was rightfully mine? I couldn't comprehend the depths of Mom's despair.

"For now," Judy continued, "getting out of 'prison' once in a while is worth it. I give Mom another week before she socks him one. Al won't see it coming."

As was her custom, Mom answered on the first ring. I wondered if she ever left her room, although Judy said Mom played bingo on Tuesday afternoons, had her hair washed and styled on Thursday mornings, and occasionally dined at a steak house with Al.

"Hi!" I sang. "Tomorrow's the big day. We'll be there around two."

"Who all's visiting?" she asked weakly.

Even though I'd repeated our plans over the course of the summer, I cheerfully recited them again: "Everyone. Gary and me, Ryan and Cara."

"Be sure to warn the kids about my memory," she quickly cut in. "What will Cara think when she finds out I have a boyfriend?"

Not divulging the fact that we had openly discussed her infatuation with men around our dinner table, I reassured her that Cara would welcome any happiness that came along.

"She has a boyfriend, too. He plays football at the high school—a linebacker, I think."

"I have gifts for Ryan and Cara, but I forgot where I put them. Judy will have to search my dresser drawers when you're here. Did you know there's going to be an auction at my house? I don't want strangers rifling through my things."

I recalled a story she used to tell about her childhood: Boarders residing on the second floor of their two-story Victorian had rummaged through the attic and disappeared with the sisters' guitars.

"That's not going to happen, Mom. Remember what Judy said? Everything will be removed and taken elsewhere for the auction."

"Oh, how sad. I can hardly see my kitchen anymore."

I could see it perfectly: louvered pantry doors, gold Frigidaire appliances, orange double sink, a bowl of ceramic fruit centered between a pair of candlesticks on the round table, and a pewter bean pot customarily filled with M&M's for our arrival. In a few days I'd be there again with Judy, only this time Mom wouldn't be holding the screen door open for us and the bean pot would be empty. I smothered the urge to share my own sadness.

"Get a good night's sleep, Mom, and try not to worry. We'll handle everything."

"Yes, I know; it's just that . . . " Her voice broke into a series of sobs, then gurgled, "I don't have anywhere else to go. No home. Nothing. I'd be better off dead."

"I love you, Mom" was all I could say.

"I love you, too, Connie. Now, remind me again: When are you coming?"

Although I couldn't place the first exchange of "I love you" between my parents and me, I'm fairly certain I was the initiator. No doubt I was in my late twenties or early thirties, after the birth of my children.

They'd come close a few times. I remember lying in the hospital bed, weakened from nephritis, and Mom gently lathering Jergens lotion on my feverish legs. She never said the words, but I knew. And each evening after Dad winked and said, "See you later, alligator," I answered, "After a while, crocodile." It was sufficient.

On the day of my college graduation, in the presence of our family and my husband's, Mom read out loud my student-teacher evaluation. Her face lit up with the descriptors *creative* and *respectful,* then beamed even brighter with the high school's decision to incorporate my poetry unit into its curriculum. Perhaps she felt more pride than actual love, but for once I didn't mind not hearing those three little words. Besides, I told myself, she wouldn't have favored an audience for a show of emotion.

A few years later, just hours after my son was born, Mom and Dad sashayed into my hospital room with the radiant air of new grandparents. Dad's "Look at him!" and Mom's joyful tears over Ryan's bassinet made my heart ache. Dad steadied my tender body as I labored to the bathroom, just as he'd steadied me seven years earlier down the aisle of St. John's. Mom lowered me into a soothing sitz bath, although I would have welcomed terms of endearment, rather than gossip from her poker club. She examined every corner of the narrow room so as not to see me naked.

Yet saying "I love you" to Ryan came as naturally to me as licking salt from my lips. I nuzzled his tiny shoulders, ran my fingers along the ruddy plane of his cheek, and vowed, "You will know my love in all ways." And he did. "I love you, little Ryan," I'd coo while guiding his toes into terry sleepers. "I love you, little Ryan," I'd sing while rinsing Johnson's Baby Shampoo from his reddish-brown newborn hair.

When I was pregnant again four years later, I wondered if I had enough love to go around. All doubt dissipated, however, when a fetal monitor recorded my baby's irregular heartbeats during labor. After my daughter hurried into the world, she was whisked away for observation and I worried she wouldn't recognize me. "Where have you been, my Cara?" I gently whispered into her exquisite, shell-shaped ear when she finally lay in my arms. "I've been waiting so long to love you."

Gradually I began ending my long-distance conversations with my parents with "I love you," feeling foolish at first with its unfamiliarity, as if trying to slip something under Mom's unflappable radar. But she noticed and dutifully responded.

I waited until the age of forty-one to hear my first unsolicited declaration from my father, during our last phone call, a couple of days before his passing. "I love you-u-u-u," he said, expanding the final syllable as if holding on to time itself. In that instant I saw his face and the features we shared: an ample nose, thick brows, tawny lips crimped with grief. I cried at the gut-wrenching honesty. It was well worth the wait.

16

Brighton Gardens rose like a white storybook castle from the surrounding lush green golf course. Weary from our early flight, we slid across the seats of Judy's car. I sucked in the August air as if it were courage itself. "Mom's thrilled you're here," she said, and I walked through the entrance with modest resolve.

It was just as she'd described. A reception desk with vases of fresh flowers hugged the left wall. Elevators were to the right, as well as a gas fireplace closed for the season. Muted blues and mauves with a smattering of yellow appeared throughout in wallpaper, carpeting, and fabrics.

I scanned the dining room, set off by a waist-high plaster partition, then the main sitting area. I spotted Mom, standing amid a crowd of chairs, craning her neck in our direction. She was radiant. As I passed the inquisitive residents gathered after their noon meal, I saw her mascara-rimmed eyes focused on mine.

"You look marvelous," I said, kissing her cheek.

"I'm so happy," she bubbled, lightly embracing me, then the others. Ryan and Cara stared at their grandmother with a mixture of joy and relief. Gary smiled and began studying the layout of the place.

"I think you're having a top-notch day," Judy said while taking Mom's arm, equally relieved with her mood and our good fortune.

"Oh, I am. Should I show them around?"

Her voice was steady as she pointed out her usual table in the dining room. Although I was amazed at the staff's efficiency, having already prepared for dinner with fresh linens and water goblets, I couldn't take my eyes off Mom. If I hadn't known better, I would have thought she was a visitor; she was dressed in her best clothes—a lilac-striped T-shirt, a lightweight cardigan, and Dockers jeans faded ever so slightly. How could this woman, with hair neatly sprayed into place and skin creamed to perfection, be the disheveled mother I'd seen just a few months before? The antidepressant she had been given to stabilize her mood must be working.

"Here's my mailbox, number 231B," Mom said in a hallway lined with rows of built-in brass containers. "Of course, I don't get much mail." She took an elasticized bracelet off her wrist and inserted one of its two silver keys into the lock. "See? Nothing today."

I peered into the empty space and swallowed hard. I vowed to stock up on note cards when I returned home. Mom had always been a huge proponent of formalized mailings. Birthdays required prompt sincere greetings, and holidays, wishes for good cheer. Even St. Patrick's Day brought cards plastered with shamrocks and cauldrons of gold. When she'd started signing them with "I love you," I'd saved every last one.

I understood the value of mail. In grade school I'd stored my hospital get-well letters in a kitchen drawer under the paper bag holding my ponytail. When I'd discovered them missing several years later, Mom said she'd followed my doctor's advice and thrown them away. He'd reasoned I might use them to garner sympathy. I felt as though my legs had been chopped off at the knees.

An elevator opened, and we were assaulted by a heavy dose of evergreen air freshener. Judy had warned me about Brighton Gardens' policy of strict odor control, but it definitely bordered on overkill. "We might as well go up," Mom said. I wondered how long I could hold my breath. The others, except Mom, looked similarly affected. No one spoke until their shoes touched the second-floor carpet.

"Wow," I said. "Nice decorations."

"Gaudy, if you ask me," Mom scoffed. Each apartment was identified by number and nameplate, and in some cases, swags of dried flowers. Wood shelves at each door displayed stuffed animals and knickknacks. Taped on the door of room 231 was an ivy-edged letterhead stating "Welcome, Virginia." The shelf alongside it was dusty and bare. Mom put the second key into the lock and carefully inched the door open, as though afraid of what she might find. We followed her into a tidy, miniaturized version of her bedroom on Palisades Lane.

"Judy brought me a few things. Of course, the bed and dresser are new, but I've got my TV, hurricane lamp, and rocker. I don't know what would have become of me it wasn't for Judy."

"We're all grateful," I said, glancing with admiration at my sister. Her cheeks and the full length of her neck reddened with the attention.

It had been a tall order to fill: moving Mom in her agitated state to the assisted-living center, decorating a space to her liking, taking daily phone calls that consisted mainly of complaints and disappointments. Although I didn't think my short visit would make a dent in Judy's burden, I planned to be as useful as possible.

Ryan and Cara gravitated to a pair of wicker chairs Judy had bought at Pier 1, and Gary sat in the rocker. My attempt at conversation felt forced yet important.

"Your bed looks so cozy, Mom. The sage-green blanket matches the walls. And there are your friends on the pillow." I resisted the urge to pick up the brown teddy bear and floppy-eared rabbit, so as not to disrupt her propensity for order. Yet it was as if she hadn't heard me at all as she began searching her drawers, mesmerized by their contents—sweaters, cotton briefs, and rows of white crew socks.

I remembered an evening on State Street when Mom and Dad had gone to a friend's house. Emboldened by their absence, I'd snuck into their bedroom and switched on a Tiffany-style lamp on the low dresser. I'd never thought to peek inside Dad's drawers. However, Mom's were irresistible, especially the top one, filled with photos, birthday cards, and, most important, my Mother's Day card. It had been a fifth-grade assignment: to print *M-o-t-h-e-r* vertically on the left-hand side and write what the letters meant to me on the right. Since Mom had given my colored-pencil sentiments top billing over all the store-bought cards, I'd felt reassured of her love.

Now I suddenly understood the purpose of my visit. It was more than offering support to my sister, more than assessing the home she'd so carefully chosen. I needed to stand face-to-face with my mother and tell her I loved her. For everything she'd done throughout my life, even if at times she'd been selfish, domineering, and downright unlikeable. As she closed the bottom drawer and turned in my direction, I felt at peace. Any lingering fear I'd had of this woman dissipated. My greatest discovery was as natural and uncomplicated as the afternoon light on the windowsill.

Mom held the steering wheel with one hand and plugged her nose with the other. My siblings and I laughed and plugged ours, too. Commercial Street, especially by the Foundry, always stunk of rotten eggs. We'd put up with it anytime for a day at Danke's farm.

The highway overpass signaled the end of town and an abundance of fresh air. We rolled the windows down and eagerly breathed a mixture of black earth and manure. Mom pulled into Walter and Lauretta's long gravel driveway off Winchester Road and said, "See you later, cowboys." I jumped out of the car and wrapped my arms around Teddy, an ancient collie with eyes diluted to the color of putty. I was certain he remembered me.

I loved Mom those mornings she set us free to explore the farm of Grandma's oldest friends. Their kitchen was the first stop. Homemade jams, breads, and sugar-crusted pies lined the counters. "Toast and eggs before you get going," Lauretta said. I'd thought we'd struck it rich.

After breakfast, her youngest daughter, Marlene, threw a fringed blanket over a pony and saddled the chestnut mare. I envied the red bandanna tied loosely around her neck, the dirt-caked boots that spoke of a life so different from mine. She helped Judy and Bill mount the mare and then pitched me up onto the pony. With one expert swoop, she was behind me. We set out for the meadow, the sun just beginning to turn the world a luminescent green. My eyes watered from the crisp air, but I kept them open, not wanting to miss one triumphal moment.

When the horses tired and heat seemed to rise right out of the earth, we cooled off in the relative darkness of the barn. Yet there was no time to waste. Bill climbed a wood ladder to the loft and spread-eagled onto Walter's neat piles of hay. After my usual hesitation, I followed and willed myself to drop. My reward was a thousand pin-pricks through my socks upon landing.

We were dead tired and smelled like sweaty horses when Mom picked us up for supper. "Have a good time?" she asked. *If only you could have seen me,* I thought. *How pleased you'd have been. Riding like there was no tomorrow.* I imagined I was a country girl well into the evening.

Mom's favorite photographs were sprinkled around her room. On the windowsill next to a thriving cactus, ten-year-old Cara posed as if gliding across ice, one white skate firmly planted and the other raised and extended beyond the flat plane of her back. I could almost hear the serene piano score of *Forrest Gump* as Cara spun gracefully in a dress of blue chiffon.

"I'm happy to see Grandma on her horse," I said, inching toward an eleven-by-fourteen frame hanging above Mom's dresser. "How old do you suppose she is?" Even though I knew the answer, I wanted to test Mom.

"A teenager. Mother was so spoiled. Selfish when she had us girls. I don't know why I have it."

Judy laughed. "Mom, you love that one of Grandma."

"I know, but now I have to look at her *every day.*" The whites of Mom's eyes expanded like eggs in a frying pan. She shrugged. "Let's walk to the Country Kitchen." She turned on the heels of her recently purchased Reeboks and opened the door. It was like old times: Mom telling us what to do, and we responding en masse. In an odd way, it felt normal and comforting.

I wondered if we'd run into Al. Although Judy had predicted that Mom would break up with him once she discovered his drinking habit, they now spent afternoons together, either in Mom's room or downstairs in the common living area. Except for a nurse flipping through paperwork in a corner office, the second floor showed no signs of life. Perhaps Mom had warned him of our impending visit and he was keeping a low profile. After all, scarcely a week had passed since he'd yelled at her at the top of his lungs during dinner. Later she'd complained to Judy, "I shouldn't have to put up with his abuse." I agreed. The last thing Mom needed was another man to spar with.

The Country Kitchen was a pleasant surprise, wallpapered and naturally bright from sunshine streaming through the sheer curtains. There was a refrigerator, a microwave, and oak cupboards. Apples and bananas rested appealingly in a glass bowl on a counter. Mom pulled out a vinyl-cushioned chair from the rectangular table and motioned for us to join her. I remembered our positions at mealtimes on State Street. Bill and Dad occupied the short ends of the yellow Formica table, while Judy sat across from Mom and me. Although the arrangement kept us at arm's length, it couldn't completely guarantee my parents' preference for quiet, civilized meals. While they ate with their heads down, my siblings and I giggled and chewed until Mom had had enough. "Can we *please* just eat?" she'd ask, spacing the words apart as if they too were incorrigible children in need of separation.

"They usually have donuts out in the morning," Mom said, and I began to attribute her recent but necessary weight gain to a fondness for chocolate long johns. Chocolate, in all varieties, had been a staple in our household: walnut brownies, cupcakes, malted milk balls, chocolate-covered peanuts. In fact, there was plenty of sugar for us kids to dip into. Although Mom was strict about mealtimes, she didn't regulate candy consumption. Our family dentist used to say, "Connie, your teeth have seen too many sweets." I didn't care—that is, until his elderly hands came toward me with a drill as loud as a jackhammer. And since he didn't believe in novocaine, I clenched every muscle in my body. At least my teeth were white and straight. Mom always claimed they made me prettier. Even during her decline, she still managed to compliment me on my teeth whenever I visited.

"Want to play cards, Mom?" I asked. "Rummy?"

"If you do. But I'm getting hungry."

"Grandma, how about a banana?" Cara said.

Mom grimaced, negating any chance of her eating a healthy snack. Worse yet, she began focusing on dinner, which was hours away. We had promised to take her to Rosati's, a local Italian restaurant she liked.

"When can we go?" Mom groaned, clearly tiring of our idle chitchat.

"Not until we play at least three games," Ryan answered, shuffling the deck. I silently thanked him for his thoughtfulness. Without my husband and children, I thought, I might remain frozen in this moment forever, only to be discovered years later by another family visiting a loved one. *Look,* they'd say, *a remarkable still life.* I'd drop my head onto the table and weep.

At Rosati's an upbeat waitress with a messy ponytail seated us by a wide window. "Hello again, Virginia," she grinned, exposing buck teeth that could have benefited from braces. Mom beamed from her chair between Ryan and Cara, looking much younger than her age.

"The buffet has great pizza," Mom said.

I recalled how often she'd ordered a medium cheese-and-sausage from Sammy's. It had been a highlight of her workweek and had become a lifelong obsession.

"So, Connie, you think I look pretty good, huh?" she asked with an uncharacteristic glint in her eyes.

"Better than good. Your hair is styled. Your blue jeans are hip. Dad would be proud."

Mom blushed like a schoolgirl. "Oh, he was so handsome when we met—a hunk. Too bad he can't see how well I'm doing."

I imagined him sitting beside her, observing silently as he'd often done. He'd wink in my direction, sip his beer, and picture his wife as a young woman. His eyes would tear up, as they had that first Christmas without Grandma. I'd reel from the unobstructed depth of his pain.

As Mom walked to the buffet, I wished my brother were here to gauge her improvement. However, he'd been married in a civil ceremony a few weeks before. He and his wife had the unenviable task of combining households that included her two daughters from a previous marriage and my nephew, who visited every other weekend. They planned to repeat their vows in her church in October. Bill had asked if we'd all come.

As Mom returned with her pizza, I wondered if she was capable of making the trip to Florida. Judy and I hadn't told her yet. "Maybe we can use the wedding as a bribe," Judy had suggested earlier. "Say we'll handle the house and the auction, and when it's over she can go with us to Bill's."

At the assisted-living center the following morning, we congregated in an open area designated "the library" because it contained a short bookcase with a handful of paperbacks. Mom was wearing the same outfit she'd had on the day before; a dried dab of pizza clung to her lilac T-shirt. I sat uncomfortably across from her, noticing her growing agitation. She rocked back and forth in a wingback chair and glanced continuously from one end of the room to the other.

"Judy, I can't live in this *hellhole* any longer," she said finally. She clasped her hands on her lap and rubbed one thumb across the other. I felt a familiar dread, as if I'd been pressed flat like an autumn leaf under waxed paper. How could Mom's behavior and opinions change so substantially overnight?

"Really," Judy said, exasperated.

"You try living here for a day. Listen to the old biddies smack their dentures at supper. It's enough to make anyone gag."

"Quiet, Mom. I've met a few of the women, and—"

"I want to go home," Mom quickly broke in.

Oh God, I thought. Was she having a moment of clarity and actually remembering her house on Palisades Lane? I was shaken by a quick jolt of remorse.

"We'll talk about this later—just you, me, and Connie," Judy said. "Now is not the time." I could practically see Judy put her foot down.

Gary, Ryan, and Cara shifted nervously in their seats. I attempted to change the subject. "It's our anniversary today. Twenty-eight years. I'm so glad we're here to share it with you."

"That's nice, Connie," Mom said listlessly. "But can you give me one reason why I can't go home?"

During the years after Dad died, Mom obsessed over the tiniest details of her existence, and everyone else's. Even my visits were subject to scrutiny.

"I'll be here on Sunday, waiting for you. And I hope Gary's family isn't plotting to monopolize your time."

I'd reassure her that a get-together at my brother-in-law's could hardly constitute a monopoly. "You're always invited, even expected to come. There's no excuse to sit home and pout." Yet, sure enough, we'd plan an outing and she'd claim disinterest. Mom worked damned hard at maintaining her loneliness.

One summer, her organizational skills reached troubling proportions. "Make a list of what you want from the house when I'm gone," she said. "I've started putting sticky notes on things."

"Why?" I asked sarcastically. "Are you planning something we're not aware of?"

She was indignant. "It pays to be prepared. If I get sick or hit by a car . . . "

I thought it was nonsense. She'd always been extremely healthy. Her chances of being mowed down while crossing the street were statistically improbable. Yet I felt uneasy the entire visit. I didn't linger too long in one room or glance at anything too closely, in case she was watching. "What about this brass platter?" she asked a few days later. I shook my head. "Maybe the tea set?" I tried not to venture any opinions.

I didn't finish my list until the following winter. I mailed a handwritten note, hoping to silence Mom once and for all on the subject.

"I'll bring the first three items with me in May," she announced over the phone a short time later.

"I don't want them *now*," I said.

"It's not much—Judy's jewelry, Daddy's stamp box, and Gen's teacup. They'll fit in my carry-on."

I reflected on my carefully composed list, the difficulty I'd had coming up with something personal. Judy's bracelet and ring were her best pieces, gleaming silver inserted with generous ovals of sodalite. Grandpa's stamp box, a gift from his parents after they'd moved to Los Angeles during the Depression, was a diminutive marvel: an enameled pagoda against aquamarine sky, hinged as if one could enter its shoeless space. I didn't know how Mom could part with it, since her own grandfather had been mugged and beaten within an inch of his life. Yet the irony was startling. The pagoda would find its way back to California, where I lived just a few hundred miles from my relatives' interment on Whittier Boulevard.

Gen's teacup was the most puzzling. Mom had a special love for Grandma's cousin and the hand-painted treasure she'd given her after my birth. It was an exquisite piece: a blue-bonneted girl clutching an iridescent parasol, her pale pink dress and white pinafore sailing around her knees on a breezy day. On the bottom of the cup, Gen had printed "Virginia, '23," and Mom had added "Connie, '52" in gilded letters. Mom said, "You can add Cara's name under ours." Now I felt anxious about the responsibility of owning it too soon. Would it survive my frequent moving? Could I forgive myself if it didn't?

"Please," I begged Mom over the phone. "Respect the list for what it is: my request for when you're no longer with us."

My pleading did little good. When I picked her up at the airport, she held her carry-on close to her side as if protecting a million dollars. I pictured her settled in my guest room, brushing her hands together and muttering with satisfaction, "One less thing to deal with."

"Bill spilled the beans," Judy said, clearly flustered, as I opened the hotel room door.

I gasped. "When?"

"Last night. He called Mom after we dropped her off."

"Well, I guess he had every right to." We plopped down on the pull-out bed. At least the room wasn't the embarrassing, clothes-strewn mess it had been before Gary and the kids had packed and left for their 8:00 am flight to California. I ran my fingers through the short hair beginning to dampen around my ears. "So, what do we do?"

"Stick to bribery. Perhaps we can get her to the wedding if she has mostly good days."

"Well, you'll end up being the judge of that after I'm gone."

Judy shot me a look of panic. "Terry thinks if we all work together, take turns . . . We've got a month to decide."

"You're right," I said, trying to convince myself. "Tomorrow we leave by ourselves to do the inventory. She'd freak out just seeing the yard."

Judy seemed somewhat calmer. I rolled over on the thin mattress and sighed into the pillow that still smelled like Ryan. "Everything's going to be okay, Jude." I hoped the words I'd asked Gary to repeat every night when we lay side by side were adequate. The mother in me wished I had more to offer.

When my children were small, Mom's mantra was "Enjoy them now; they'll grow up all too fast, then leave forever." Although I'd assumed she'd wanted my siblings and me to speed up the process, I was astounded by her sincerity. I often wondered if she'd been as satisfied as I was to simply trim tiny toenails or comb cornsilk hair. I wasn't always convinced.

Yet Mom was the first person who came to mind when I recalled my hospital stay at age eight, or an outburst of boils before that. How loving she'd been, lifting me onto the kitchen counter and singing softly into my ear while she drained pus from each boil. When I shrieked with pain, Judy fainted onto the linoleum. Mom wiped her brow and said, "What next?"

I'd had a similar, dual crisis with my own children. One afternoon Ryan fell from the slide in our backyard, hitting his head on a euca-lyptus stump. I carried him into the house, laid him on the couch, and asked how many fingers I held up. He answered correctly but seemed to be drifting away. I left him in the living room with eighteen-month-old Cara and called the pediatrician from the phone in the kitchen.

As I listened to the nurse's instructions on how to treat a possible concussion, I was aware I didn't hear Cara. "Can you please hold on?" I asked. I rushed back to the living room, where Cara was helping her-self to a mouthful of dirt from an African violet. "Good Lord!" I bel-lowed, scooping her up while considering the toxicity of houseplants. I ran to the bathroom, yelling, "Ryan, keep your eyes open!" Cara fought me tooth and nail over every speck of dirt I managed to scrape off her tongue. Then I remembered the nurse on the other end of the line.

"Is everything all right?" she cut in when I began apologizing.

"I'm not sure. One kid is almost unconscious, and the other's prob-ably poisoned."

Whenever I retold this story, I thought of Mom. She'd bend over double with images of Judy and me and say, "How did I ever live through that?" Then, in a more serious tone, she'd add, "It's what you did. Took the good with the bad and tried to do right by everybody, no matter how hard it was." Perhaps Mom had viewed her roles of wife and mother as worthwhile challenges. Perhaps she enjoyed her children more than I'd realized.

I took my own duties of motherhood quite seriously. I knew how it felt to be the child on the receiving end. "Girls are to be respected and never harmed in any way," I emphasized to four-year-old Ryan when his sister was born. When Cara grew old enough to recognize and take advantage of the vulnerable human spirit behind male toughness, I explained, "Boys have feelings, just like girls. Wouldn't it be wonderful if you could be fast friends all your lives?" She found this hysterically funny, as if I were proposing she stand on her head and juggle nectarines at the same time.

Ryan babysat his sister a few hours every morning the summer she turned five. I'd return after lunch from my part-time job and hear his report: "She didn't get dressed until *ten thirty*."

Then he'd add with self-satisfaction, "She ate half of her peanut butter sandwich and a few slices of pear."

"He wouldn't let me leave the table!" Cara chimed in.

Sometimes they'd barely notice me walk in the back door, so intent were they on constructing a Lego city, complete with Lego people and Matchbox cars. I'd wished that could have been Bill and me twenty-five years before. He built a water wheel with his Erector Set while I watched from the sidelines. I marveled at its tiny motor and maze of colored wires. He hadn't asked for help or thought to say, as Ryan had, "One more block here, Cara, and we'll have another house."

I was one of the few mothers who hated to see their kids go back to school each September. "Time to myself without all that bickering," a neighbor would say. Although I'd heard plenty of late-summer "I'm sick of yous" between Ryan and Cara, I still honored requests for tuna salad sandwiches or a trip to the movies. Our days were full and as colorful as the fruit-flavored gummy bears they devoured. Even if Mom's mantra hadn't been "Enjoy them now," I'd have done so instinctively. I craved the closeness of a loving family.

17

Judy and I packed her car with clothes and food for our four-day stay at Mom's house. Although it was only August, the trees in her yard bore traces of the season to come, a yellowing in the breeze, quickly appearing and disappearing, like butter blending into warm chocolate. I reluctantly settled into the passenger seat.

"You forgot to show me your garden," I said sadly, suddenly remembering the rope-framed plot in the backyard. She had followed in Dad's footsteps by growing string beans, tomatoes, onions, and zucchini.

"You're not missing much. It's overgrown and weedy."

Her voice was melancholy as she clicked her seat belt for the short ride to our first stop, Brighton Gardens. "Things will settle down," I said. I thought about sinking into Gary's arms and walking my dog to the park; I knew I had the better end of the deal.

Mom wasn't in her usual chair on the first floor. "Odd," Judy said. "It's almost lunchtime."

We took the elevator up and knocked on Mom's door. She opened it with a huff. "I've been waiting for you two."

As she walked toward the bed, we slid into the wicker chairs across from her.

"Judy, why do you have to go? Who will take care of me?"

I could tell she'd been lying down. There was a neat groove in the center of the sage bedspread. Her pillow was propped against the nightstand; she hadn't slept on one in years.

"Connie can't close up the house by herself. She needs her fun and talkative sister to make the job more interesting."

"The *job*? It's going to be that much of a chore?"

Judy's smile faded, and her eyes widened. "Well, yes! We have to go through everything." I nodded in agreement.

"I'm glad I'm not going," Mom said, glancing out the window. "I can't take any more stress."

"Why don't I call Betty when we get there? Where is your address book?"

I pictured the tattered, spiral-bound notebook still resting in its nook in the secretary.

"No, Judy," Mom sighed. "I haven't talked to her in a while."

"I'm sure she'd want to know how you are," I offered. Betty was her lone friend from the printing company. She lived on her own, even though she had health problems. "A tough old lady," Mom claimed.

I waited a minute before breaking the silence. "We have to leave, Mom. Walk us down on your way to lunch?"

She glared at me as if I'd asked her to trek through the Alaskan wilderness. "You won't be back, will you, Connie?"

I knew a quick good-bye was our best recourse. "I'm always with you, okay? We'll talk over the phone." I kissed her cheek, smelled the cream she'd applied that morning, and felt my legs move toward the door.

"Do you know how *long* Miss Sauer made me stand at the blackboard?" I said, fuming, as a friend and I trudged home after school. "I hate algebra."

Within seconds, a tremendous noise pierced the winter air. I whipped around and saw one car sliding sideways across the icy street and a long line of others attempting to brake. Doors flew open, and a flurry of mothers ran toward the curb. I gasped when I spotted the center of their attention: a motionless child face-up in the gutter. They rubbed her cheeks and bootless feet, but she didn't respond. Where was *her* mother? I wrapped my scarf more tightly around my neck. My bare knees knocked together. When the ambulance arrived, all the boys and girls who had stopped in their tracks quietly moved on.

I could barely tell the story to my parents. As they stood horrified in our warm kitchen, I realized they imagined my body splayed on the frozen ground. *I'd have called out for you*, I wished I could say. *To hold my weightless hands, to stroke my deadened arms.* I'd never want to feel so alone.

When I was older, I wondered how I'd react upon seeing my parents laid out on cream-colored folds of satin. Mom didn't care to be "shown"; of course, I knew I'd have to see her up close, touch her unblemished forehead.

Dad had wept over Grandma's casket. After she was buried, he talked more to my siblings and me. Mom said it was because we'd grown up. "You three were all hustle and bustle, overwhelming most of the time. It's easier for him now." I thought she overlooked the fact that he'd lost his father, mother, and sister; besides Florian, we were all he had. We became the new focus of his attention, and it was wonderful.

"We forgot these photographs," Judy said in the guest room on our last day of the inventory.

I laughed as I stood face-to-face with my seventeen-year-old self. "Look at my pageboy, perfectly shaped at the jaw." I winced at the memory of sleeping on wiry brush rollers attached to my head with bobby pins.

We took the frames off the wall and carried them to the kitchen table, where we'd piled other last-minute items: a half-used bottle of Chanel No. 5; peach bath towels with price tags still attached.

"Did I ever tell you about the last time I saw Sister Thomasita?" I asked.

Judy unplugged the coffeepot. "No. What made you think of her?"

"Well, she wore her habit in the nursing home, but she looked all wrong. Her beads were twisted at her waist, and gray hair stuck out of her cap. She didn't know my name or how we were related."

"Eerie," Judy said, dumping the grounds into a black Hefty bag we'd propped by the back door.

"I concluded God had played a cruel trick on one of his faithful.

Now I don't think He had anything to do with it. Dementia is in our genes."

Judy turned and peered at me over her eyeglass frames, which tended to slip down her nose. "Sister wasn't the only one, Con. Grandpa had it, too."

"What?" I dropped into the closest chair.

Judy slowly continued while shifting her gaze to the window. "I was eleven. Rita answered the phone. Grandpa had been found wandering downtown, she said, and who was going to pick him up?"

I felt blindsided. Mom had recounted all the hideous details of everyone's illness—Aunt Cele's cancer, Grandma's schizophrenia. Why not this? I'd known only that Grandpa had been short, semibald, and terribly reserved. Suddenly I needed to understand everything: what to expect in the coming years, how long it would be until Mom didn't recognize us. If I had been home, I would have googled "Alzheimer's" for the hundredth time. I imagined myself growing stronger by the minute with experts at my fingertips.

While Judy wiped the counters, I headed to the bathroom for one last shower. The air was still steamy, even though she'd cracked the window after hers. I stepped out of my pajamas and into the gold fiberglass stall, then ran the water extra hot. I pictured Dad sudsing his broad chest in the room directly below me and remembered what Cara once said: "Because you saved Grandpa's life, I had a chance to know him." Now I tried to conjure up images of them together in the first nine years of her childhood, but I couldn't. All I saw was my own grandfather, floundering along the sidewalks of Main Street. Who had saved him?

When I was growing up, we had more photographs of the Kennedy family than we did of our own. Judy had compiled a scrapbook of newspaper clippings after the President's assassination.

In my own collection, I had two photos of Grandpa's family. In the earlier one, dated 1920 and taken after the older sons returned from the war in Europe, both great-grandparents and their eleven children stared dolefully into the camera. Emery and Al, the youngest boys, sat cross-legged on the floor. Although they weren't twins, everything about them was the same: crooked noses, knee-length pants, and high-top leather shoes. Behind them stood two rows of siblings who bore little resemblance to one another, except that the remaining five brothers were stiffly dressed in three-piece suits with wide lapels.

I often tried to find my mother's features in this family. Only the thin line of Grandpa's mouth and the serious gaze of his oldest sister, Ann, reminded me of her. What was astonishing, however, was the remarkable resemblance to family members of my generation. Sister Thomasita (not yet a nun in this portrait) had the heart-shaped face and wide eyes of my cousin Becky. The youngest girl, Germaine, with a gigantic bow framing her pulled-back hair and high forehead, could have easily passed for either Rosemary's or Rita's daughter. And Ann looked strikingly similar to Judy, with full lips and a tilted head, a pose Judy often struck in photographs.

Ten years after this photo was taken, the family moved to Los Angeles, except for Sister Thomasita, Germaine, and Grandpa. Of all the siblings, I wanted to know Ann. "She's the only one who writes," Mom used to say. "Her life sounds so appealing. She's single, supports herself. Perhaps I'll visit someday." Travel consisted of destinations within a two-hundred-mile radius of home; Mom didn't make the trip until I'd moved to California.

I had few pictures of myself as a child. One was from my birthday party when I was five. My friends and I had been playing "drop the clothespin in the milk bottle." I was petrified at being the center of attention and stared straight into the camera, my body as stiff as the gingham encircling my knees. Of course, the entire party was difficult. "Speech! Speech!" Sharon cried out at the table. Mom said, "Connie, stand and tell everyone how happy you are that they came."

I shifted uneasily in my chair and took off my pink paper hat, certain I'd faint or throw up. Thankfully, my friends let me off the hook, returning to their chocolate cake and Kool-Aid. Yet I wondered if I'd ever be like them: comfortable on my own two feet, which were sweaty and tight in my saddle shoes. I wondered how it felt to be brave.

I zipped my suitcase on the guest bed and took a final look around: orange velveteen chair, beige Princess phone, notepaper stamped boldly with the logo of Twin Cities Savings and Loan. I heard Judy sigh in the hallway, one of those long expulsions of air we'd both perfected in the last few days. "Ready, Con?" I silently wheeled my bag through the kitchen, then plunked it down the steps into the garage. Judy locked the dead bolt behind us.

I stood on the crumbling concrete and smelled the trash we'd double-bagged, the cord of wood my cousin Scott had agreed to take, the accumulated dust from the last years of Mom's life.

A final good-bye always smacked of abandonment. Since rejection had been one of my childhood fears, I didn't want to pass it on to my kids. I was especially vigilant about not making them ever feel left behind. Yet the summer Cara learned to swim—a four-year-old, slapping chlorinated water with gurgles of delight in a blue-and-white-striped suit—I felt as though I was deserting her when we drove away from the Disneyland Hotel. And when we'd left the Residence Inn in San Diego the month before Ryan's tonsillectomy, I had the urgent need to run back to our room and guard the boy on the pullout, whose raspy, old-man breathing had kept us up all night.

Every time I signed my name on a real estate transaction, I felt as though I was abandoning people I loved: the dirt-poor college couple who watched *Saturday Night Live* on a twenty-inch black-and-white TV in their third-floor walk-up; the family of three who took afternoon naps side by side on the caramel shag rug of their fixer-upper; the growing family of two kids, two parakeets, and a shih tzu who breezed out of their suburban two-story as if they'd never lived eight years under its wood shake roof.

Judy tapped the automatic garage-door button, and we walked out, turning to face the dark-brown house Dad had stained the year before his cancer. "This is it," I said, glancing around at every last detail. Cobwebs hung from the eaves like patriotic bunting; I pictured the new owner eventually brushing them down. The evergreens needed pruning, and crabgrass squeaked through cracks in the driveway. We finally pulled up the hot silver handles of the car doors and crawled in.

"I have to toughen up," Judy said, rolling down her window.

My eyes stung. "You're tough enough."

It didn't occur to me to scrutinize my own strength. I'd handled adversity in the past, and I just assumed I could do it again.

Judy looked over her shoulder and slowly backed the car down the driveway. As we turned onto Highway P, I could have sworn we'd left our mother behind. I didn't think I'd ever comprehend Mom's loss. But I did know this: Her life had been peeled and sectioned like an orange. Dementia would devour all of it.

18

"Safe trip," Judy said, hugging me tightly as the westbound train screeched to a stop in Naperville.

I couldn't answer. Her heart pounded against mine, and I knew this was the closest I'd ever get to feeling mothered.

Because I still wasn't flying since my long bout of vertigo a few years before, Amtrak was my method of transportation. I loved everything about train travel: sunrises and early-morning breakfasts of bacon and eggs; afternoons to read novels and write poetry; chicken or steak dinners, followed by occasional card games in the lounge car; and, of course, the scenery. No matter how many trips I took along the same route, I always found something new to catch my attention.

But most important, I didn't have to be "somebody" on the train— not a boss, a wife, a daughter, or a mother. I had no responsibilities other than feeding myself and getting a good night's sleep. And without the encumbrance of a telephone, I was unavailable to the outside world. I doubt I'd ever felt as free as when I boarded the California Zephyr.

This time, the coach car was crowded and stuffy. I wheeled my bag through a vacuum-sealed doorway to the next one, grateful I'd spent a few hundred dollars more on a sleeper. The room was designed for two people, with lower and upper berths, yet I couldn't imagine sharing it with anyone. The "closet" was as slim as the gap between my refrigerator and cupboard back home. Since I slept next to the window, I'd have to get up every time the person above decided to get down. I wouldn't volunteer for that spot, either; I'd be claustrophobic with the beige cloth ceiling inches from my face.

The following afternoon, I stepped onto the platform in Denver. The air was refreshingly dry compared with the humidity I'd left behind, and I drank it in voraciously. With a thirty-minute stop for refueling, I entered the long line for the pay phones.

"How's it going?" Gary asked—his question no matter if I walked in from the next room or called from a thousand miles away.

"I'm tired. One more day."

"Ryan's watching baseball. He's driving to Santa Barbara Monday, although he hasn't packed yet. Cara's walking Jack—or, rather, she's standing with Jack while talking to Joey."

I pictured them: Joey, our next-door neighbor and the object of Cara's recent infatuation, four years older and ruggedly handsome; Jack, sitting patiently on the sidewalk; and Cara, in a tank top and denim shorts, holding Jack's leash and looking at Joey in the besotted manner she'd adopted at the beginning of summer.

"Well, I wish Joey didn't have so much free time. Have the boxes arrived?"

"Yesterday. Hopefully UPS repacked your mom's stuff better than we did."

"Could you check? I don't want to come and—"

"Don't worry," he cut in. "Everything will be fine."

Of course I'll worry, I wanted to say. I'd have done anything to protect the little I had left of Mom's world.

The train pulled into Glenwood Springs, just over the Rockies. A group of teenage boys mooned us from an adjacent road, and I began to feel my mood shift. Across Interstate 70, to the left of the track, was the old-fashioned, redbrick resort I'd dreamed of visiting. I yearned to be one of those carefree women lounging poolside. I'd sip a glass of chardonnay, page through a magazine, and cool off in the dazzling water.

I remembered zipping down DePere Street on my Schwinn as a kid, with a beach bag embellished with dolphins slung over the handlebars.

At the Jefferson Park pool, I changed in a curtained dressing room, took the mandatory shower, and made a running dive into the five-foot end. When I was out of breath, I lay on hot, gritty concrete. It was heaven.

Everyone in my family loved to swim, except Mom. "I never had the opportunity," she'd say, "and I'm afraid of water." Scalding air temperatures couldn't entice her to dip her toes.

Dad, on the other hand, charged into Green Bay like a catfish. Even at sixty, in the pool of our rented townhouse, he swam laps and played alligator with two-year-old Ryan, sinking, surfacing, and finally scooping him onto his back.

The train jerked forward again. Every scene through the glass-domed observation car led me back to Mom: the Colorado River rushing through the canyons, the junipers and ash lining its shore, even the subtle hint of autumn.

I remembered gathering hickory nuts with Dad every fall at High Cliff. We'd find them scattered beneath a damp layer of leaves by wind that swept the ridge above Lake Winnebago. Once we were back home, in the basement, Dad cracked them with a hammer and I picked out the sweet meat. Mom meticulously cut the pieces with cuticle scissors, stirred them into bubbling chocolate, and baked batch after delicious batch of brownies, dusted with powdered sugar. We relished every morsel.

When the conductor announced the first seating for dinner, I jumped at the chance to share a table with people who had their own stories to tell. I never underestimated the power of distraction.

My mother-in-law was the grand dame of storytelling. She'd proclaim the pale Easter-colored Victorians in San Francisco magnificent, then reminisce about her own cramped childhood home by the Fox River. A loving mother and distant father became as real to me as if they were sitting beside us in the van.

I enjoyed Bev's stories and looking through her scrapbooks. "Here I am," she'd say, fingering the crisp, yellowed corners of a black-and-white photo of her in a nursing-school uniform, with friends she'd kept track of for fifty years. She'd point to another and recall raising her children on a parcel of land in the Palisades before neighbors crowded in: Gary as a toddler, with his pet chicken tied to a sapling, and his two spritely sisters, bundled in snowsuits. Unlike my mother's sad recollections of her own life, Bev's were wonderfully vibrant. She shared them with anyone who took the time to listen.

It came as no surprise to me when I realized I'd modeled my family after Gary's. I learned the absolute importance of affection and laughter from my in-laws. Even times of crisis, mentally exhausting and serious, could "make or break us," Bev used to say. "I never got so low that I couldn't pull myself up." Although not as efficient, I preferred to think that for the most part I'd done so as well.

During Cara's recovery after fracturing a vertebra, I picked up her homework at school. I thought our troubles had expanded exponentially when the science teacher handed me a dead frog preserved in formaldehyde and plastic. "You'll only need a paring knife and toothpicks to see what's in this guy."

At home Cara raised her thinly plucked brows disapprovingly and balked at the injustice of it all. I studied the outline of the metal brace beneath her sweatshirt and offered the services of her father. She trudged off to the garage as if granted a stay of execution.

I retrieved jackets, since the spring night was exceptionally chilly. Gary set up the card table. The three of us stared at the frog, pinned and stretched like cloth in an embroidery hoop.

"I'm not . . . I can't . . . ," Cara stuttered.

Gary winced. He positioned the knife over the hard, moss-colored belly and cut.

"Oh my God!" she screamed when its contents became visible. "Don't squeeze," she added hastily. "You might move something important."

"Like what?" he laughed.

"I don't know. We have to examine its stomach and liver. *You* touch it—you have a glove on."

Gary glanced at me, then obeyed. "I'm guessing these were flies . . . and the liver is smooth, slimy, like Jell-O."

"Cool," Cara said more confidently. "Now, where are the intestines?"

Quietly I stepped away from the table. Determined to be useful, however, I went inside and got the camera. Although the image was seared into my brain, I thought I'd need proof for anyone who might doubt our story.

Gary centered his truck on our driveway, and I slid out. The landscape had that two-weeks-away feeling—familiar yet noticeably different. Ivy climbed the stone wall alongside the front steps, but now bright green tendrils sought direction, drifting this way and that in the breeze. Even the lavender separating our yard from the neighbor's seemed thicker.

I parked my suitcase inside the garage and opened the door. Jack was trembling with excitement on the landing. He licked my nose, and I scratched briskly behind his ears, knowing he'd ignore me later as punishment.

It was a typical Sunday. Newspapers were strewn across the coffee table. Preseason football blared on the TV while Ryan miraculously slept on the sectional. When Cara ran out of her bedroom, my world felt complete.

"*Mom!*" she cried, curling into my arms. "Thank God you're home. Ryan wants to order pizza again. How are you? How's Grandma?"

I savored the smell of her coconut shampoo. "As well as can be expected. Is there anything in the refrigerator?" I held her with that long embrace she'd come to accept, an unwillingness for release that usually made her giggle.

"Let's double-check," she said.

That evening I called Judy and told her I was home. "It's not the same without you, Con. I saw Mom yesterday. She was out of Coke, so I took her a twelve-pack. She's one sour little apple, though."

"In other words, she's her normal self."

"Exactly. Al knocks on her door with the tip of his cane, which drives her crazy. Her roommate gets up three times a night to pee, and Mom can't fall back asleep." Judy took a breath, then chuckled. "But *this* is priceless: She asked if we found anything unusual in the house, anything that made her look bad."

My mind raced to Mom's bottom dresser drawer. "What did you say?"

"I said, 'Do you mean something like a red satin nightgown?'"

"I wish I could have seen her face, Jude."

"She claims she never wore it and that's why it was still in the bag. Yet she *might* have if the occasion arose."

The image of Mom wearing lingerie in a color she'd tolerated solely at Christmas went against everything I'd known about her. Not once since Dad had died had she given us reason to suspect she had any interest in another man. Yet I wondered how different her life could have been. Although speculation seemed pointless, it was preferable to picturing her now: sitting alone on a twin bed, cursing the steady tap of an old man's cane.

"Virginia, want a beer with your pizza?" Dad asked.

"Well, why not? I'm on vacation."

I was surprised at Mom's good nature on the first night of their visit. Usually by dinner she'd still be upset by the airline's inability to serve a decent meal, or by the man who'd coughed continuously in the seat behind hers on the four-hour flight.

"Grandma, do you really drink?" Ryan asked skeptically, as if she'd just agreed to throw back shots.

"Now and then," she answered.

As Dad signaled our waitress, I reminisced about the few times I'd seen her drink. While playing cards, she'd have a Tom Collins; with a Friday fish fry, a draft beer. I'd concluded long ago that her conservatism was due to the extended family's tendency to overindulge.

"This is a great place on a weeknight," Mom said, brushing her shoulder against his. I was amazed at how the small gesture touched me. They rarely sat close together.

As we ate our pizza, I decided there had to have been a spark between them all along, a silver ray of hope that survived in their household for almost fifty years. I remembered a photograph of them when they were young, nestled in a corner of Grandma C's sofa. It must have been a special occasion. Mom wore a satin dress with a deep V neckline. A crystal pendant glistened against her skin. Her dark hair, smoothed behind her ears and dipped slightly onto her forehead, caught the light of the camera. I'd thought she could pass for royalty with her head tilted, smiling demurely into the distance. Yet, holding a cocktail on her lap and leaning into Dad's chest, she was as relaxed as I'd ever seen her. Confident and satisfied. Loved.

Dad had his arm wrapped around Mom. He focused on the dress cascading past her knees, and a broad grin creased his angular face. I imagined his fingertips stroking her bare skin when the picture was snapped—so taken with her, he'd forget the cigarette between his left fingers and stumble to tap its ashes before they fell onto the carpet.

I often thought their happiness had been sealed, along with the picture itself, between the plastic sheaves of my photo album.

After I talked to Judy, I wasn't sure I had enough energy to finish unpacking. My natural tendency to return things to their proper order won out, however, and I emptied my suitcase. The trip felt longer than the pile of dirty clothes suggested.

I finally made my way to the guest room, where Gary had stacked Mom's boxes. With new resolve, I cut the packing tape on the largest one, knowing it was my brother's bookcase. I remembered my astonishment upon discovering it in a corner of Mom's basement, and my even more surprising urge to rescue it. Besides the Candlewick dishes, nothing connected me to my childhood as much as this, the altar Bill once prepared for the Virgin Mary.

Again, I pictured us kneeling before her: Judith Ann, William David, Constance. When I asked my parents why they'd given me a nonbiblical name, Mom explained her admiration for Constance Bennett, a glamorous blond film star who'd entertained troops in Europe. When I asked why they hadn't christened me with a middle name like my siblings had—or anyone else I knew, for that matter—Dad said Constance was long enough for a little girl. I agreed but felt strangely different from my friends. "No middle name?" they'd say incredulously, as if I had one eye missing from its socket.

Gary stood in the doorway. "Take a break."

"Not yet. I've been cooped up for days."

Together we opened the remaining boxes and unwrapped the items I had so carefully chosen: the blender for Ryan; a blue blanket and windup doll for Cara; a brass soup ladle, whisk-type eggbeater, and cookie cutters; a portrait of me in my wedding gown, posed on an ornamental bridge in Smith Park with autumn oranges and yellows nearly artificial in their perfection; and the Pepsi bottle Mom had filled with water and sprinkled over clothes before ironing. I could almost see steam rising from hot cotton.

"One casualty," I said sadly, placing an oval pewter container in the palm of my hand. "The lid is missing." Because of Mom's fondness for pewter, I'd given it to her one Christmas with pearl studs ensconced in its velvet lining. The lid, with a gold, long-stemmed rose overlay, had made the piece. Without it, the container looked like a cheap trinket for loose change. I didn't have the heart to keep it.

"That's enough for now," Gary said firmly, leading me by the arm to the family room. I felt an unusual sense of relief and relented.

Ryan and Cara were lying on opposite ends of the dark-blue sectional, entranced by the A's game. Through the window, I noticed the sun creeping up the valley. While I'd been gone, the toast-colored eastern hills had been transformed to amber, a reminder of the Oakland fire nearly a decade ago. Now I worried about the common area behind our property line; with the ever-present wind, the dry weeds would make superb tinder.

"I need a minute," I said, heading for the back door.

Although the patio was shaded, the thermometer still read ninety degrees. I slipped off my sandals and sunk my feet into the lower pond of the waterfall. The water was tepid at best. A potato bug lay on the bottom, eerily skeleton-like, with outstretched legs. I saw the hill above me purpled with rosemary, the oleanders hanging on to the final blossoms of the season. *This is what one does,* I thought. *Hang on, even when the last thread seems about to break.*

19

"There was entertainment at the home," Judy told me one Sunday evening in September. "A trio in their seventies, on sax, keyboard, and drums, playing all the old songs. Mom was enthralled with the saxophonist in his black turtleneck. 'That's a guy to die for,' she whispered."

I laughed. "Well, did she at least like the music?"

"I'll say, although she wouldn't do the hokey-pokey, not even to get his attention. 'He doesn't know I'm here.' I told her she blew it. And, believe it or not, I kept a lookout for Al."

"Do you think he'd be jealous? Is Mom after every man who comes along?" Even though Mom and Al still spent time together, I didn't think their relationship would amount to much.

"Well, there aren't too many to choose from, but she knows them all. It gives her something to do, since she refuses to socialize with the women."

I recalled a warm July night when my friends and I staged a production in Pam's backyard. We'd practiced our acts for days—puppet show, baton twirling, and dance revue. We assembled costumes and sold tickets to neighbors in advance. With lemonade and store-bought cookies, we anticipated a night of stardom.

My dance number was a solo. Having chosen the role of a mysterious gypsy, I swayed beneath Mom's discarded flowered skirt with an unaccustomed confidence, the violet cotton swirling luxuriously around my legs. When my accompanying music dropped to a soft, slow finale, Mom asked from her seat in the audience, "Connie, how much longer? We're being eaten alive by mosquitoes."

I nearly fell off my high heels from embarrassment. Afterward she offered obligatory niceties to the ladies and hurried home through the backyards as if something vitally important awaited. I promised myself then and there that I would strive to be a different kind of mother—one who actually enjoyed, and took an active interest in, her children's activities.

The auction had been slated for two weeks after I returned home. Unlike the summertime weather still suffocating our valley, I imagined the chill in the Midwest air, maples rushing to achieve the vibrant reds of maturity, gray squirrels gathering food to last another season. I was certain Judy was just as eager for life to resume its normal rhythm.

I was thankful I wouldn't be in attendance at the downtown warehouse. The idea of Mom's silverware and plates, knickknacks and wall furnishings under scrutiny made me queasy. Even though Judy claimed she'd be fine without me, I wasn't sure if she was being entirely truthful. I wondered if I'd ever know.

The only personal stories my mother shared were those about hard times. She had an extensive repertoire from which to choose, since every decade brought more grief.

When we'd drive by her childhood home on Forest Avenue, before the graying two-story was razed, Mom would remember Grandma's reclusiveness as "a sick kind of selfishness, for which we all paid dearly." Gripping the wheel, she'd recall every lurid detail of Grandpa's passing in the parlor, how blood spurted straight up in the air from an artery that burst in his neck. I'd say, "Surely there must have been some redeeming moments," but Mom would bristle and drive on. I didn't believe she realized that she was steadily following in her mother's footsteps.

The first home my parents owned, by the now-abandoned railroad depot, had been equally trying. "When your dad switched on the basement light, rats vied for position on his shoulders. I thanked God the day we got out of that dump." If she had experienced anything akin to a young bride's joy, she never mentioned it.

But it was the stone house on State Street where I grew up that caused Mom the most heartache. Three children, Dad's drinking, Bill's dropping in and out of college. Even the move to the Palisades—"starting over, with everything new"—didn't purge her memories. She'd relive one abhorrent episode after another as if nothing else mattered. I'd say, "Oh, Mom, we had fun, too." She'd look away in disgust.

"Bill, when are you going to stop puffing your life away?" Mom asked through the screen door as he and I stood on the driveway. Her voice carried the same scathing reproach as Father Joe's during confession.

Bill shrugged and stamped his cigarette thoroughly into the concrete. "C'mon, I've got something to ask you."

We brushed past Mom and descended the basement steps to where he'd recently taken up residence. With another semester beginning in less than a month, and without much money left from his travels, he'd moved back home, scattering his belongings in the "green room," since Mom had dismantled his boyhood bedroom and christened it the "den."

Her initial reaction to Bill's decision to live in our house again had been "You're going to do *what*?" Then she'd reasoned, "Maybe *this* time you'll stick with it and get a diploma." A college education was the standard of achievement; we were, she often reminded us, "the first generation with the means and opportunity to attain it."

Bill pulled a string hanging from the ceiling and flooded the room with light. "I don't have any cash to buy you a wedding present. I'd like you to choose, from my limited possessions, your gift."

I was startled by his frank admission on the day before my ceremony. But as I sat beside him on his unmade bed, a mattress encased in a wrinkled, threadbare sheet, I understood. I followed his serious gaze around the room, honored by his request. Among piles of clothes, books, and record albums on the floor and coins in a beer mug on top of a stereo speaker, I saw, at best, two possible items.

"I got that in Tijuana," he said, pointing proudly to an onyx chess set.

"Must have been expensive."

"Nah, they got truckloads of them. But it's a beauty."

I tried to picture my longhaired brother haggling with a Mexican vendor, but it was a scene from a world as distant to me as the crown of a cedar to an earthworm. And although Bill had patiently taught me the strategies of knights and rooks, it was a game I hadn't quite mastered. I didn't think the chiseled white or cobalt figures would improve my skill.

"I do have Judy's painting," Bill offered with a trace of uncertainty. *The Three Faces* was propped against the wall, its deep-green and gunmetal acrylics melting into each other with abstract abandon. Yet there was a definite sense of elongation—cheekbones, we'd thought—and the black elliptical shapes they encompassed stared fiercely at their observers. The brooding canvas was Judy's best work.

"Are you sure?" I asked.

"I wouldn't offer otherwise," he said more assuredly. Looking down at his tanned feet, he added, "An excellent choice."

I was astounded by Bill's generosity. Yet as I carried the painting to the compact Chevy that Gary had bought for our honeymoon drive to Mackinaw Island, I wondered if Bill would regret his decision. Guiltily, I wedged it into the hatchback while debating where I'd hang it in our tiny apartment. I felt worldly in the true sense of the word, with an unfamiliar joy of ownership and a shockingly deep love for my brother.

I felt flushed and distracted the day of the auction.

"Why don't you try reading for a while?" Gary suggested. "Or we could grab lunch and go to a movie. It will be hours before Judy calls."

I shook my head. "It's so goddamn horrible," I said, pacing the kitchen, my bare toes discovering crumbs I'd missed during my earlier, haphazard sweeping.

Gary rested his hands on my shoulders. "Your mom will get through this. She's a tough old woman."

"Yeah, she's tough all right, on *us,* with her blistering tongue: 'Why are you doing this to me?' 'You want to watch me suffer.'"

I noticed Gary's tired face and realized we both needed a break from current events and my ranting. Gary had taken on more responsibilities in my absence, and I was trying to catch up at work and at home. Our alone time had suffered. I welcomed other subjects to talk about besides my mother. I gave him a hug and picked up the newspaper on the counter. "So, what's playing this weekend?"

I had just removed one leg from a tubful of lukewarm water when the phone rang in the bedroom.

"I've been waiting all day," I said breathlessly upon hearing my sister's voice. I sounded more anxious than I would have liked, but the afternoon had dragged. Even Cameron Crowe's depiction of himself as a young journalist during rock and roll's heyday in the film *Almost Famous*, with music I'd listened to since I was a teenager, felt long and indulgent.

"The auction was weird, Con," Judy began. "Maybe twenty people, including us. Tom worked hard on the presentation—kitchen items grouped together, linens—so everyone could get a good look. I'll tell you the grand total first: fifty-two hundred, after his percentage. I'm convinced it would have been more if the auctioneer hadn't rushed. Then again, we didn't have the big pieces of furniture the buyer kept for the house."

"Every dollar counts," I said, hoping to bolster her spirits. "Besides, now it's over and you get to go home—"

"And find places for the stuff I bought."

I thought I'd misheard her. "*You?*"

"Well," she said, somewhat defensively, "since we kept the rocker for Mom, I couldn't let the matching vanity stool go. That cost me forty-five bucks."

I was astonished. It had never occurred to me that Judy would buy back Mom's things. She hadn't voiced an interest in anything else a few weeks earlier.

"I paid twenty-six for the brass coffeepot," she added casually. "So altogether I spent two hundred and fifty."

"Did the others buy stuff, too?"

"Rosemary and Marion added about a hundred dollars to the cause.

Rita picked out a couple of small items. Bev was the only one who went home empty-handed. She seemed upset. I'll admit it was unnerving, with those yellow paddles going up and down. But, Con, there were things I just couldn't part with."

I didn't completely understand the motivation behind their purchases. Perhaps they couldn't resist the bargains. Maybe they wanted remembrances of Mom. Yet the irony of Rita owning some of Mom's household wasn't lost on me. I had always hoped that Rita was oblivious to the fact that Mom failed to regard her as family.

I stared at the clouds forming in the night sky outside my bedroom window, a swarm of gray ovals like the smoke rings Dad used to exhale. What would I have done if I'd been at the auction? I saw myself hunkered at the back of the room as if it were my girlhood closet, my eyes squeezed tight, dry like day-old lemons, my ears plugged by fingers greedy to stall the terror in my world. I wouldn't have bought a thing.

"They wheeled out another lady last night," Mom said when I called the next morning. "During a thunderstorm."

"Well, the seasons are changing," I said dumbly, trying to sideswipe the real issue.

"Then I wondered if I'd left my wedding dress hanging in my closet."

Relieved to be back on familiar yet muddled ground, I said, "No, I didn't see it."

"Oh well. Did I get rid of it?"

"Probably." *Although if she had an ounce of sentimentality,* I thought to myself, *she'd have given it to one of us.* I glanced at my parents' photograph on my dresser. Dad was twenty-four, remarkably handsome in his wool Navy uniform. Mom was twenty-one, and even though fresh snow dusted the brown grass beneath her feet, she smiled warmly in her long-sleeved white gown. Dad's arm encircled her tiny waist in the infancy of their marriage, yet unspoiled and rich with possibility.

"Are you looking forward to Bill's wedding?" I asked, hoping to distract her.

"Connie, I don't know if I can go."

I cringed at the bewilderment in her voice, the same skepticism she'd expressed four months earlier, before her scheduled flight to visit me. Selfishly, I thought about how I'd redeemed her United ticket for Tampa, and the plans Judy and I had made for what we hoped would be a smooth trip.

"Besides," Mom continued nervously, "I'm constantly running to the bathroom. How can I do that on a plane?"

"We'll just get out of our seats and go. Either Judy or I will take you."

"What if you *lose* me?"

I stifled a callous urge to snicker. "Mom, that's not going to happen. We'll be so close together, you'll probably get sick of us."

"Never," she said emphatically. "You two are the only people who care."

Mom had always been brutally honest, but this time I knew she was wrong. "That's a very sad way to look at things. Think of all the people who've helped you. We'll have a good time with Bill. I'm sure he's excited to see you."

Actually, I wasn't certain at all about my brother's feelings. When Judy had told him we were bringing Mom, he hadn't responded one way or another. "Dead air," she'd told me. "All I got was dead air."

Mom sighed. "Okay, I'll go. But what will I wear?"

I sensed our problems were scarcely beginning.

20

Gary, Cara, and I flew to Tampa at the end of October. Unfortunately, Ryan was in the middle of a semester in Santa Barbara; I'd miss his easy way with his grandmother, his natural ability to make her happy.

The weather matched Bill's description—hot, humid, and postcard-perfect. We settled into a Holiday Inn near his house and unpacked. Within minutes our clothes acclimated, feeling damp to the touch on metal hangers.

"Let's take advantage of a free afternoon," I said. "It might be my only one."

We changed into our swimsuits and flip-flops and headed to the pool. With a few hours before Judy, Terry, and Mom arrived from Chicago, and before we met Bill and my nephew, Brian, for dinner, I didn't intend to waste one glorious, sun-filled minute. I set my sights on a chaise lounge, hoping to fall asleep, since I'd failed miserably on the plane.

"Get wet first," Cara suggested, arranging her fuchsia towel on the chair closest to mine, with an air of teenage importance. "Then we'll be really tan for the wedding." Having momentarily forgotten the purpose of our visit, I said, "Not yet." I bunched my terry cover-up into a pillow and lay down.

"Mom," she insisted, but I held my ground, in this case the discolored vinyl straps of the chaise. I drifted into that luxurious state of mind brought on by heat and the heady scent of chlorine.

From what seemed like miles away, I heard her skip across the blazing concrete and dive smoothly into the water. The truth was, I needed more than a few minutes to lull my overworked brain. For the past several weeks, I'd anticipated every conceivable scenario of our family reunion. Since Judy and I had already established our upcoming roles—I would be Mom's primary caretaker during the day, and Judy would handle evening duties, including sharing a room with her—I planned to remain in a prone position until sunburn, heatstroke, or both threatened me.

My thoughts wandered to our visit thirteen years earlier, for Bill's first marriage. We'd stayed at Alpaugh's, our parents' chosen spot from previous vacations because of its beachfront access to the Gulf of Mexico. Like experienced tour guides, they'd shown us around: our one-bedroom suite, a worn yet accommodating space for Ryan and Cara to amass seashells and souvenirs; a courtyard stocked with palms, hibiscus, and a resident blue heron; and their second-floor, corner-room view of the water, clearly the most desirable in the lodge.

Mom's recently permed white hair appeared above my paperback. I watched her grasp a handrail and carefully descend the steps to my staked-out spot.

"I asked you to wait for me," Judy called breathlessly from twenty feet away. Her cheeks were stunningly bright.

Mom shrugged her shoulders, still sweatered from what I presumed had been an overly air-conditioned ride in the rental car. "Connie's right here," she answered defensively. My stomach churned as I rose to hug her.

"You made it," I said against her perspiring hairline. I knew my simple greeting, even without the usual questions of "How was your flight?" and "Did you wait long for your luggage?" would elicit a predictable, pessimistic response. I took a deep breath and held it.

"I told Judy maybe the trip wasn't such a good idea," Mom shot back. "Help me get this damn thing off, will you?"

I pulled the cardigan from her arms and noticed her pallid face, eyelids collapsed from exhaustion. "Only positive thoughts allowed,"

I said, exhaling renewed determination. "After all, how often do we get together? Look, there's Cara." I pointed to a bobbing figure in the middle of the pool. Even though I waved and yelled, she was unaware of our presence, methodically gulping air and cutting water. More than ever, I needed her calming effect on her grandmother, a finely honed ability I envied.

"No one cares if I'm here," Mom said dejectedly. "So can we finally get out of the hot sun?"

As I gathered my belongings, I remembered how their relationship hadn't always been comfortable. "She's *mean*," Cara decided as a ten-year-old. "She says I'm fatter than when she saw me last. Do you think I'm fat?"

I tried to reassure her. "Of course not, and Grandma doesn't either. She meant you're growing, filling out."

Cara couldn't let the matter drop. She'd study her profile in the mirror and frown at her tiny bump of a belly. "There's pressure on young girls these days to be thin," I reminded Mom. "Cara's pretty sensitive."

Somewhat deviously, Cara fought back. Knowing her grandmother's displeasure with the aging process, she'd state with surprised seriousness, "There's a dark spot next to your eyebrow." Mom would straighten defiantly, then laugh. "Must you *analyze* me?" Cara thoroughly enjoyed getting a rise out of her.

Judy unzipped the suitcase she'd packed for Mom, and I was startled by how little it contained—a plastic bag of toiletries, a nightgown, socks, jeans, and T-shirts. She pulled out a denim dress and said, "Remember this? I thought Mom could wear it, instead of me guessing at her size."

I didn't mention that I saw the loose-fitting garment every day in a photo hanging above my dresser. Judy had worn it two summers before when we'd posed for a family portrait at the mall. Mom had been resistant. "*Why* are we doing this?"

"Because we're all here," I'd answered, "even Bill and Brian."

Now I was reminded daily of when Mom's behavior had become

noticeably different, when simple requests were met with hostility and our presence increased her agitation.

"It doesn't matter what I wear," Mom said, rolling her eyes.

"Do you have shoes?" I asked cheerfully.

She winced. "I don't know, Connie. I want to lie down." She shuffled over to the first double bed and claimed it.

Judy dug into a suitcase pocket and retrieved a squashed pair of navy pumps and panty hose. Sensing my hesitation, she said, "They're better than nothing, Con. Her attire tomorrow will be the least of our worries."

I agreed yet couldn't help but compare Mom's new look to the one she'd carefully chosen for Bill's first wedding—a stylish blue silk dress and eggshell open-toed heels. Even though it was too late to take her shopping, I wondered if Bill would be disappointed.

Her face, however, was still unblemished and youthful. No matter how busy she'd been when I was growing up, Mom had always paid strict attention to her facial regimen: a morning cleanse with Noxema, followed by moisturizer and a dab of foundation for work, and another Noxema wash at bedtime, along with a thick application of Eterna. "This stuff works wonders," she'd say, and I was a believer, although under the bathroom fluorescent, her skin appeared as greasy as bacon. It seemed like an unpleasant price to pay for maintaining one's appearance.

Judy tapped my arm, and I followed her out of the room. "Some peace," she sighed heavily. "I hope Bill appreciates this. Mom's come a long way."

I knew exactly what she meant. "No matter what happens tomorrow, she's done her best; we've done our best." I looked away as she raised her hand to wipe a tear. At this point, strength was all we could count on.

I drifted on a thin air mattress thirty feet from the sand of Peninsula State Park and wondered if the conversations in my head would ever stop. They played over and over with the irritating scratchiness of old cassette tapes. Although twenty-three and married, I was still incapable of controlling the din.

"What's done is done," Gary had said the night before, as we'd snuggled in sleeping bags inside our canvas pup tent. "Your mom and Bill can't get along, so maybe it's better that he leaves."

"What if he never comes back?" I whispered, staring into the numbing darkness.

Now, as occasional waves from distant powerboats rolled beneath me, I thought of my brother's decision to pursue the life of an artisan on the road.

"I'll make some big bucks," Bill had said excitedly, "with all the mirrors and planter boxes I finished over winter. Hell, I'll see more of the country."

His enthusiasm wasn't contagious. My idea of a good job included an eight-hour workday and an employer-signed check. His dream of traveling from one shopping-mall craft fair to another sounded financially risky at best.

Mom took it the hardest. "Why can't you just stay with one thing? All that money your dad and I forked out for college . . . What a waste."

"I'll finish," Bill argued. "Just not now."

These arguments between them always made me think of a nursery rhyme: "Wednesday's child is full of woe, Thursday's child has far to go." I had been that Wednesday girl, born with overwhelming sensibilities. As a Thursday product, Bill seemed destined to never live up to our parents' expectations. Then I recalled a second, newer version of the rhyme: "Wednesday's child is loving and giving, Thursday's child works hard for a living." Perhaps it was silly and superstitious, but I realized anything was possible. I swam ashore, determined to leave my girlhood behind and anticipate the letters Bill promised to write.

We waited for Bill at a restaurant known not only for its delicious seafood but also for the huge mallets it supplied patrons for decimating crab legs and lobster tails. Our sandals crunched peanut shells and bones into the tile as we were shown to a picnic-style table.

"I remember this place," Mom said, sitting on one of the benches. "Bill brought us here. People lined up clear out the door, waiting to get in." She glanced at a group of guys sharing a pitcher of beer, at a family of boisterous towheaded boys. One in particular caught her eye, and she smiled. For the first time during the trip, she seemed to be enjoying herself.

"Hey," Bill laughed from somewhere behind me. I turned and met his open arms, bronzed and muscular. Except for the cigarette habit he'd been unable to kick, he appeared to be the epitome of middle-aged good health.

As he greeted everyone else around the table, Mom gushed, "Bill, you look wonderful."

"Well, so do you."

For a few seconds, we were comfortably silent. After months of turmoil and cross-country phone calls, we'd pulled it off. I had never doubted our loyalty as siblings, unlike Mom, who had often said we'd probably drift apart as adults, the way so many other families had. She'd even made the bold claim that after her death we'd fight over her belongings like alley cats. The fact was, we trusted each other the way some people trust God. I hoped Mom realized that before it was too late.

Bill kept his word. Week after week, I'd open the tarnished brass mailbox in our apartment lobby and find envelopes with the return address "B.C., many miles away." I realized that while I was studying poetry in redbrick college classrooms, Bill was living it: postmarks from Syracuse, Baltimore, Sioux Falls; postcards from Wyoming, Colorado, Utah, and Arizona. For a woman who'd crossed the state line three times, his day-to-day life was nothing short of magical: sleeping under the stars in the vastness of country I'd never thought I'd see for myself, navigating snow-tipped mountains, chopping wood for heat and planter boxes.

Although his correspondence stretched my imagination, I couldn't fathom the loneliness he spoke of. He traveled and worked with a friend or two. He savored women. But he said he missed the things he'd tossed aside when he'd packed Thunder (the nickname he'd given his Pontiac) with books and record albums for the final time:

consistency and stability. I envied his freedom, but not the sense of the unknown.

I saved Bill's letters in my top dresser drawer. I added his Christmas greetings and birthday cards and held them together with a thick rubber band. Over time it dried and cracked and I replaced it. When Gary and I moved from our apartment to a condo, then eventually to California, Bill's correspondence went with me.

Mom perched stubbornly on the edge of her bed, refusing to dress for the wedding. "I can't bend down and put on pantyhose," she moaned. "*You'll* have to do it."

I glanced hesitatingly at her unshaved legs. Although only her calves would show beneath the hem of the denim dress, her swollen feet needed the slip of nylon to slide into her shoes. "Try," I said grudgingly.

Mom remained frozen, with her arms crossed, reminding me of Cara when I'd told her to drink milk as a child. Sometimes a tablespoon of chocolate Quik would convince her; I didn't have any tricks up my sleeve for the belligerent woman in front of me.

I squatted on the floor with the pantyhose in my hands. As I approached her left foot, I was struck by the strangeness of dressing a parent. We'd had little physical contact over the years, nothing to prepare me for this intimate act. I'd never touched this part of her body before; the skin was shriveled and dry. Again I was the girl who needed to do the job right so as not to cause disappointment. My fingers felt large and clumsy. I was afraid of running the nylon or, worse yet, poking a hole clear through it.

"You're twisting it around my leg," Mom complained when I'd finally made some headway. "Oh, just let me do it."

I was grateful to be relieved of the duty. I watched her undo my hard work, then pull up the pantyhose with ease, as if no time at all had passed since she'd done it.

"You conniving sneak," I said. She nearly smiled. I threw back my head and laughed.

21

We parked in one of the few shady spots in front of the Baptist church. Even though it was October, the air was thick and heavy. Cara appeared older than sixteen in her spaghetti-strapped sapphire number. While Gary endured a summer suit, I was determined to stay as cool as possible in a sleeveless dress.

Our family felt incomplete, however, without Ryan. I'd miss his tenderness toward Mom, the way he could take her mind off herself. I remembered the first Christmas after Dad died. She sat sullenly and alone in a corner of our living room, staring at nothing in particular and oblivious to how her mood affected all of us. "Grandma," Ryan said, with that I-won't-take-no-for-an-answer look on his face, "I've got the cards and pennies, so let's play poker." He bounced across the Berber carpet with his usual self-assurance, certain of whipping all opponents at the game his grandparents had taught him when other boys played Go Fish.

"Well, that's just what I need," Mom answered, miraculously following him to the table.

As I squinted into the high afternoon sun, Bill and Brian pulled up behind us. They wore identical white shirts and black slacks and shared a feature that proved they were father and son: a smile as wide and bright as their coveted stretch of Honeymoon Beach. At fifty-two, Bill was as handsome as ever, and I was struck by how much he carried himself like Dad, shoulders squared under his suit jacket, arms loose at his sides.

"Big day!" I said.

Bill shook hands with Gary, then adjusted his round titanium glasses while looking at me.

"You being here makes it even bigger."

I was as thrilled as when I'd first realized we'd become friends. Gary and I had driven from Milwaukee to Bill's apartment in Green Bay. Over pretzels and Budweiser, we discussed everything: school, money, dreams—especially dreams. We tried to picture where we'd be in ten years, what we'd do if we had a million dollars. Gary and I fantasized about owning a home on the lakefront. He dreamed of a Porsche for weekend excursions, while I wanted a car more practical for the family we planned. Bill also had his eyes in the sky, but he longed to travel the continent—from one mountainous end of Canada to the other, from the Atlantic Ocean to the Pacific—in search of open sky and beautiful women.

Gary, Cara, and I joined the others in the first pew. Judy and Terry smiled, but Mom seemed completely lost in thought. I glanced at Bill, positioned now beside his best man at the foot of the altar, and Brian directly in front of them. At eleven, Brian was a miniature adult, composed yet methodically tapping one polished black shoe as if summoning the newest family members to appear. And they did: eight-year-old Sarah, full-skirted in ivory lace and carrying a flower-girl basket; Meghan, the same age as Brian, yet a foot taller, and quite womanly in floor-length teal satin; and, on her stepfather's arm, Laura, dazzling in a scoop-necked white dress and a single pearl pendant echoing those on the bodice.

As tapers flickered and the service began, I remembered my own candlelight wedding. On a brutally humid August evening, Dad escorted me down the red-carpeted aisle of St. John's. Just before we reached the Communion rail, I kissed his cheek and caught Mom's watery eyes. It was the closest I'd get that day to a declaration of their love.

I turned now toward Mom, slouched and somber, and realized that a show of affection would probably elude my brother as well.

Bill and Laura carefully slipped gold rings onto each other's fingers. I admired their decision to give marriage another shot. After all, wasn't reaching out to another person instinctive? Didn't self-preservation demand such effort?

It was so clear to me now what had been missing in my mother's life. Even before the onset of dementia, she'd stopped trying to help herself. It was as if she'd maneuvered through childhood and adulthood with hopefulness and longing, then retreated into a cocoon, thick-skinned and almost impossible to penetrate. As Brian sang a tribute to the couple in his boyish soprano, I felt as if I'd been tossed a buoy. Time was irrevocable; I'd make the most of what I had and be thankful.

"Don't leave yet," Bill said after the ceremony. "We need you for pictures."

I took Mom's arm, staving off her escape into the crowd. "Pictures," she scoffed, slumping onto a pew with an appreciable *hmpf*. I nudged Gary, the official photographer, to get started, uncertain of how long we could keep her occupied. I tried my best at small talk. "So, Mom, what do you think they'll serve at their house?"

Mom narrowed her eyes until they were mere slits. "*Their* house?" Her voice was shrill, and I wondered if it echoed through the church with the same intensity as it did through every vein in my body. "It's *Bill's* house."

"God, Mom. Shhh!" My pulse quickened beneath my clammy skin, my elbow ready to jab her if necessary. The obligation of keeping her quiet was like trying to subdue an obnoxious child seated between guests at a dinner party. Although embarrassed, I was not intimidated. This time, my brother deserved to be spared.

The interior of the light jade house smelled as if someone had been cooking for days: a blend of delicate citrus and ginger and heady foods of substance, stewed beef and sautéed vegetables. I detected sweet coconut and lemon wafting from round silver trays on a side table in the dining room.

"There's certainly plenty to eat," I said cheerfully to Mom.

She seemed puzzled by her surroundings, as if she'd never been here before. Many things had changed. Now a piano hugged the wall beneath Judy's giant silhouette of a hippie couple. Sofas covered in a Southwestern print, clearly the domain of Laura's three cats, dominated the living room. When Mom glimpsed the wood shelves holding her beloved pewter, she exhaled a deep breath of relief and flopped into one of the folding chairs added for the occasion.

Judy and I sat on either side of her as guests streamed in. The smoking contingent, including Bill, headed for the screened back porch. Part of me wondered if he was consciously avoiding us. I couldn't wait for him to break away and visit with Mom.

"Hello, Virginia. I'm Laura's mother." The petite woman who extended her hand to Mom was genuinely warm. I was touched by her gesture, and so was Mom, who beamed broadly, as if that had been her mood all along.

"How nice to meet you," she said politely, commenting on the lovely wedding and spectacular weather. I was dumbfounded by her quick-change artist performance. After others introduced themselves, then moved on for appetizers, Mom rolled her crafty eyes and asked, "Well, how did I do?"

It wasn't the first time I'd witnessed such theatrics. When I was in high school, she volunteered to take me to an opera at the community college, for which I'd receive extra credit. On the way, we stopped at Waverly Beach to pick up my friend, who bolted from her house like a horse at the starting gate. Then I saw why—lake flies, thousands of them, black and big-bodied, sticking to our windows like gum on concrete. Mom switched on the windshield wipers, which made matters worse. "We'll never get out of here," she said with a clear note of panic. She inched the car forward, but even that proved risky. Finally, she turned off the ignition and we sat. Checking my watch, I knew we'd miss the first scene.

Minutes passed before the swarm finally vanished. Mom opened the glove compartment and reached for the ice scraper. I almost started to snicker but caught myself. She attacked the scum on the windshield until an arm-sized swath of light appeared.

The Marriage of Figaro was in progress when we arrived. As we settled into our seats, Mom smoothed her dress over her knees and whispered, "What marvelous costumes." She was riveted. You'd never have known she'd just battled the plague.

Around seven o'clock, we gathered to watch Bill and Laura slice the wedding cake. I'd always been amazed by how such a simple tradition managed to quiet a crowd, as if it were witnessing a lifesaving operation. Now, as dessert plates passed reverentially from one hand to another, I felt honored to be included.

It was easy to see how Bill had been drawn to this family, to Laura's nurturing parents, aunts, and uncles. Sheer numbers alone attested to future successful holiday gatherings. He wouldn't have to spend another Thanksgiving eating a TV dinner or come home to an empty house on Christmas Eve after working the late shift at the hospital. There'd be more than enough loving arms and hearts to support him.

"Since Bill's here, I'll get Mom's present," Judy said quietly.

A surge of anticipation ran through me. I remembered when we'd set aside Mom's hand-painted plates a few months before. Each one depicted a different fruit—apple, pear, blueberry—and their edges were scalloped and peach-colored. "The consummate wedding gift," Judy had concluded. "Personal and artistic." Mom had agreed. We bubble-wrapped the eight-piece set, then shipped it to Florida with an admonition printed in red block letters next to the address label: "Do Not Open Until Your Wedding Day."

When Judy returned, Bill cheerfully pointed to Laura. "Let her do the honors."

Mom snapped to attention as Laura unwrapped each plate. "Making the trip was gift enough, Virginia. But these are lovely—aren't they, Bill?"

He nodded and thanked Mom. She sat taller in her chair, seemingly quite pleased with herself.

Laura repacked the plates and excused herself to check on the kitchen. Bill tagged along, detouring to the back porch, where the party continued under a smoky haze. I was stunned by the quickness of it all. The moment for Mom to bask in the glory of gift giving was over. Neither she nor Bill had offered each other more than politeness. I glanced at Judy and saw in her eyes the disappointment I was feeling.

I'd expected so much more. Not a gushy mother-son reunion, but at least an attempt at conversation after they hadn't seen each other for well over a year. I couldn't understand why Bill hadn't taken a few minutes to sit beside her, tell her how terrific she looked after everything she'd gone through, ask what her favorite meal was at Brighton Gardens. Yet, I reasoned, this was his special day. He was doing what he was capable of. Since he'd had more than his share of scalding commentaries in the past, why chance a confrontation? As an experienced psychiatric nurse, Bill knew all too well the unpredictability of dementia compounded by depression.

Of course, Mom didn't approach Bill, either. She never moved from her chair except to get an initial helping of food and go to the bathroom. Now Sundowner's cast a pall over her. "How long do we have to stay?" she asked. "I need my medicine. Isn't it time to go back to our room?"

Judy took Mom's hand and held it between hers. "Soon. Don't worry, you're with us!"

Mom pulled it back quickly, as if she'd been bitten. "Should that make me feel better?"

I couldn't help but smirk at her implication of our incompetence. Judy chimed in and threw her arms exaggeratedly into the air.

"And must you two always find everything funny?"

It was a rhetorical question we'd heard many times. Yet I was grateful for its familiarity as I tried to downplay the last ten minutes. I had an overwhelming and even childish urge for a do-over. Hadn't we learned the lessons? To make the most of each precious moment on this earth? To forget—and most certainly forgive—what we deemed as wrongdoing?

We hugged Laura good-bye in the kitchen. Bill walked us to the front door. Grinning youthfully, he said to Mom, "My turn to visit. You can show me your new place."

Her eyes filled rapidly with tears. "I'd like that. You'll be surprised," she added with a slight lilt in her voice. "I live in a shack—"

"Oh, right," Judy cut in.

"Well, I do have a friend. His name is Al. But the rest of them . . . ugh!" She stuck her nose in the air like a spoiled teenager.

"Mom!" I scolded, although I was beginning to laugh.

"Bill can see for himself. I've got nothing to hide."

With that, I stepped outside. The moon was full and angelically white. I imagined it bathing my valley at home, the shadowy yards, the headstrong current of creeks. I took one last look behind me and was startled by the rare sight: Bill's arms wrapped around Mom, her long fingers gently patting his shirt. One would have thought harsh words had never passed between them. Old hurts vanished like dreams upon waking.

As Mom cried softly into Bill's right shoulder, I knew I'd never understand her. For most of my life she'd been unreadable, the workings of her mind obscured by an invisible veil. I wanted to know what she'd kept hidden—her passions, aspirations. I wanted to know what she did with the love we offered. I'd learned to live with what she gave me, but I craved a great deal more.

My throat narrowed, and I breathed with a roaring urgency. It was too late for everything. Alzheimer's promised to strip Mom's mind like corn from a cob.

"I'm still here," I'd say.

"For how long?" she'd answer.

I'd press my lips to her forehead, quiet her thumbs that nearly rubbed each other raw.

Epilogue

My mother resided in assisted living for eight years. During that time, Judy and I witnessed the slow, steady progression of Alzheimer's. It robbed Mom of all cognitive thinking and memory, as well as speech and bodily functions. I was consumed by sympathy and compassion for her.

My final visit was in April 2008. Although Judy had warned me of our mother's drastic change in appearance since I'd seen her the previous fall, nothing could have prepared me for what I saw. Mom was slumped in a tall, upholstered chair with her head tilted to one side. Her eyes were sealed. Her jaw was clenched. The beautiful white hair that had caused her so much worry all her life was limp and unbrushed. The nails she'd kept trimmed were jagged. Traces of milk or juice, which the aides tried to get her to drink, dotted her navy cotton sweater. I kissed her cheek, pulled up a folding chair beside her, and cried.

Two nights later, while lying in a hospital bed, Mom opened her right eye momentarily. I spoke to its dove-gray iris. "You can go," I whispered. "I'm here, I love you, and you can finally go."

She passed away at six o'clock the following morning, five minutes before my arrival. I was grateful her suffering was over. She was at peace.

I returned to California after her funeral and to the third draft of this memoir. I questioned whether I had the perseverance to finish the arduous revisions. How could I concentrate on snappy scenes and logical structure when I'd just lost my mother? Could I maintain the tone, pacing, and arc of the narrative? And, most important, would I be able to continue portraying the true nature of the characters? I wasn't sure.

What carried me through was the reward of having seen Mom and Judy become friends. After years of power struggles and ill will, their relationship had blossomed. My sister was an excellent caretaker, visiting Mom two or three times a week. She monitored her eating, medication, and overall health, and she relayed that information to me in frequent phone calls. Not once did she accuse me, or our brother, of failing to help, even though distance prevented our direct participation. More often than not, she felt overwhelmed. But who wouldn't? Our mother was her unflagging self almost to the end. Yet Judy learned how to coax a smile onto Mom's lips and how to turn that smile into a full, guttural laugh. It wasn't always possible, but that came with the territory of Alzheimer's.

I buckled down with the book. It was like returning to an old friend; I pledged the attention and devotion it deserved. It was also cathartic. Old emotions surfaced, and I responded with more tenderness toward my mother and myself.

After all, I had changed as well. Now I understood how much I loved her. I had expected as much from her as she had from me. And while I had tried to be the perfect daughter, I had yearned for a perfect mother, too.

I also realized how fortunate I was as an adult to have broken free of Mom's isolating tendencies. The friendship of people, especially women and other writers, provided the nurturing I'd never experienced as a child. Furthermore, I felt empowered by my passion for travel and adventure. When I'd envied the women who were poolside at the Glenwood Springs resort from my seat on Amtrak a decade earlier, I had known the possibility of visiting in the future was very real. After my mother passed away, it became even stronger.

This knowledge propelled me forward. With a nod to everything I'd learned, including the value of human dignity and self-worth, I was determined to tell our story.

Acknowledgments

I wish to express my sincere gratitude to my mentor, Ellen Bass, who was with me every step of the way, challenging me to dig deeper and supporting my every effort to present this book's characters with truth and dignity.

I also want to convey grateful acknowledgment to my fellow writers in my Wednesday-night group and Ellen's Thursday-afternoon class. During early drafts and subsequent final copy, they listened intently, critiqued intelligently, and provided boosts of encouragement when I was in desperate need of them.

Many thanks to my astute editor, Annie Tucker, whose attention to detail and constructive advice greatly improved the finished product.

Finally, I want to thank my children, Ryan and Cara, for teaching me patience and offering unconditional love.

About the Author

Constance Hanstedt is an author, poet, and business owner living in Northern California. Her poetry has received numerous awards and has appeared in the *Comstock Review, Calyx, Rattle,* the *Naugatuck River Review,* and many other literary journals. Her poem "Ode to Beige" was published in Diane Lockward's *The Crafty Poet* (2013), a collection of poems, prompts, craft tips, and interviews.

Don't Leave Yet, How My Mother's Alzheimer's Opened My Heart is Constance's first book. It was a finalist in the Pacific Northwest Writers Association memoir competition in 2011.

SELECTED TITLES FROM SHE WRITES PRESS

She Writes Press is an independent publishing company
founded to serve women writers everywhere.
Visit us at www.shewritespress.com.

Her Beautiful Brain: A Memoir by Ann Hedreen
$16.95, 978-1-938314-92-6
The heartbreaking story of a daughter's experiences as her beautiful, brainy mother begins to lose her mind to an unforgiving disease: Alzheimer's.

Where Have I Been All My Life? A Journey Toward Love and Wholeness
by Cheryl Rice $16.95, 978-1-63152-917-7
Rice's universally relatable story of how her mother's sudden death launched her on a journey into the deepest parts of grief—and, ultimately, toward love and wholeness.

Don't Call Me Mother: A Daughter's Journey from Abandonment to Forgiveness by Linda Joy Myers
$16.95, 978-1-938314-02 -5
Linda Joy Myers's story of how she transcended the prisons of her childhood by seeking—and offering—forgiveness for her family's sins.

Green Nails and Other Acts of Rebellion: Life After Loss by Elaine Soloway
$16.95, 978-1-63152-919-1
An honest, often humorous account of the joys and pains of caregiving for a loved one with a debilitating illness.

A Leg to Stand On: An Amputee's Walk into Motherhood
by Colleen Haggerty $16.95, 978-1-63152-923-8
Haggerty's candid story of how she overcame the pain of losing a leg at seventeen—and of terminating two pregnancies as a young woman—and went on to become a mother, despite her fears.

The Coconut Latitudes: Secrets, Storms, and Survival in the Caribbean
by Rita Gardner $16.95, 978-1-63152-901-6
A haunting, lyrical memoir about a dysfunctional family's experiences in a reality far from the envisioned Eden—and the terrible cost of keeping secrets.

CPSIA information can be obtained at www.ICGtesting.com
Printed in the USA
BVOW08s1153300315

393567BV00001BA/1/P

9 781631 529528